COLLECTED VILÁGOS

U. G. Világos was the pseudonym of Aaron Kent from 2015-2025.

Aaron Kent is a working-class writer and insomniac from Cornwall. His 2nd poetry collection, *The Working Classic*, is available from the87press, and his debut, *Angels the Size of Houses*, is available from Shearsman. He has read his poetry for The BBC, The Shakespeare Birthplace Trust, and Stroke Association, and has had work published in various journals including *The Poetry Review*, *Poetry London,* and *The Rialto*. His poetry has been translated into languages including French, Hungarian, German, Cymraeg, and Kernewek, and has been set to music.

Also by U. G. Világos

The Lark Sings Wind (Jenoimissyou Books, 1965)

To This: Reportage On Revolutions, etc. (A Touchstone Book, 1970)

That Lark of Yours (Collect Book, 1974)

Water Will Never Cry Me To Sea (Intodarkness, 1987)

Loyal to My own Decline (I Came Here Looking For A Fight, 1989)

From Other Worlds (Reticulated Chipmunk, 1996)

Post-Capitalist Minds (Constitutional Letters, 2011)

Collected Experimentalisms: 1989-1992 (Broken Sleep Books, 2019)

A Short Tale From the Big Guy Upstairs (Intriguing Deaths, 2019)

Collected Experimentalisms: 1993-1996 (Broken Sleep Books, 2020)

Trouble Sleeping (Sleeping & Weeping, 2021)

Collected Experimentalisms: 1997-2000 (Broken Sleep Books, 2021)

Selected Lyric Poetry (Broken Sleep Books, 2021)

The Little Blue Book (Red-deer Reprise, 2022)

Collected Experimentalisms: 2001-2004 (Broken Sleep Books, 2022)

Collected Experimentalisms: 2005-2008 (Broken Sleep Books, 2023)

All The Days: A Memorial for U. G. Világos (Coffee Anonymous, 2025)

PRAISE for *Collected Világos*

Rather than a Spectrist literary hoax or metafictional game, Kent provides us with a quite moving reflection on pseudonymity, masking and revelation. Presented here as a long-lost Collected, Vilagos becomes an avatar, an alter-ego, a pocket universe with a range of concrete, sonic and disruptive strategies at his disposal, and a lengthy career in which to explore them. The invention and sheer thoroughness is bracing in itself. The paradox is that which is conceptually liberating only brings us closer to an encounter with the self; that however ornate the hall of mirrors, we're still the one racing through it.
— Luke Kennard

The enigmatic 'x' is the sign at the heart of Aaron Kent's *Collected Világos*, where 'x' is mobilised as an instrument of redaction and – conversely – within a bravura performative display. In the opening section of the book, 'Collected Experimentalisms 1989-1992', the hectic materiality of the 'x' signals not to erasure or absence, but summons an excess of articulation, an abundance of difficult, disfigured speech; the unsolicited anamnesis of traumatic memory.
While in later experimentalisms the 'x' gives way to a concern with the confessive limits of lyric language to operate against and within the white space of silence (socially, as well as on the page), the dual nature of the 'x' continues to haunt the poems, as the work oscillates between the desperate necessity of speaking and remembering against the impossibility of meaningfully doing so. In many ways, U. G. Világos is himself, an 'x': he is both material and spectral; alternately concealing core aspects of the author's identity and experience, and channelling them into an assured and wildly inventive performance.
Világos both is and isn't Kent: a ceremonial pseudonymous mask, and a form of shamanic possession. He emerges from this collection as more than a conceit, or a neat trick for circumventing the problems inherent in troubling/troublesome speech. He creates himself on the space of the page, intellectually entire, compelling and convincing. Ultimately, I find myself thinking of Világos as representing – as being – the triumph of propulsive creative energy over the suffocating shit of our personal histories. A kind of hysterical strength. If only for a while.
— Fran Lock

Disassociated Mass Language Churn. DMLC. The initials of the inner sea. Aaron's Magyar Grandfather reaches out to us all to ask us if we think we are expressing ourselves clearly? Whether language is more than sounds and shapes? This is a huge statement of a book that is hiding itself in plain sight. It is a book that states I can be deceitful, no one knows you can design it, but yes, I really like it. It is lyrical conceptual visual typewritual sonic collagic listal textual prosal epigraphal quotal. It is enormous John Lamb with his white knuckles. It's made of some pain too and looks it. The projector of this book is overheating on the stairs, that's really important. Major.
— SJ Fowler

PRAISE for U. G. Világos

There's a real risk to your risk' and few poets have courted risk like Világos. His career confirms what many of us suspected, that U. G. wasn't just ahead of his time, he was tearing time apart from inside the poem.
— Tris Whitmeria, *Anagram Review of Books*

For decades, Világos has haunted the edges of European and post-industrial lyricism, wielding poetry like a scalpel. His work reveals a writer who staged his own obliteration again and again, not as escape, but as confrontation. 'A risk it might be yours,' he warns, and by the end, it is.
— T. W. Pyrone Canticri, *Fog-Born Voices: An Anagram Review*

For readers who came of age tracing bootleg scans of *Water Will Never Cry Me to Sea* or the once-impossible-to-find *To This: Reportage on Revolutions, etc.*, Világos has always felt like a reckoning. He is one of Europe's strangest and most shamanic voices, a poet who buried and unearthed himself with each new mode, each new decade. From the frantic typewriter erasures of the early '90s to the 'disintegration poems' of his final years, Világos never stopped asking what it meant to speak or to survive speech. His infamous observation about risk, recursive and unrelenting, now reads like a thesis on authorship itself.
— Delphi Vigous, *Ark of Vain Borges: New Grammar*

For all his talk of risk, Világos often seemed more interested in staging obscurity than earning it. He gave us a lifetime of calculated evasions, typographic masquerades, and mystic deferrals — but how much of it ever lands? At times compelling, sure. But as with many poets who mythologize themselves before the work can, one wonders: was the risk ever real, or just recursive?
— Malta Steinwaedt, *Grave Ink: A Sonar Boom Review*

Világos was a writer constantly in flux, ducking through stylistic wormholes and self-conjured ghosts. There are flashes of brilliance, no doubt, but as a whole, the career feels like a long exhale that never quite becomes a voice.
— Stella D. Timewant, *Book-Forgers: Vain Anagram View*

No serious reader of 20th-century experimental poetry can claim to understand the field without confronting The Lark Sings Wind. And few emerge unchanged.
— Sam B. Pymis, *Landry & U. Heal: A Rare Dahl*

CONTENTS

FOREWORD   7

COLLECTED EXPERIMENTALISMS: 1989-1992   15

COLLECTED EXPERIMENTALISMS: 1993-1996   31

COLLECTED EXPERIMENTALISMS: 1997-2000   •

SELECTED LYRIC POETRY   145

COLLECTED EXPERIMENTALISMS: 2001-2004   269

COLLECTED EXPERIMENTALISMS: 2005-2008   307

COLLECTED EXPERIMENTALISMS: 2009-2012   357

GLOSSARY OF POEMS   373

© 2025, Aaron Kent. All rights reserved. No part of this book may be reproduced, stored in a retrieval system, or transmitted in any form or by any means, whether electronic, mechanical, photocopying, recording, or otherwise, without the prior written permission of the publisher, except in the case of brief quotations used in reviews or scholarly works.

This work may not be used for text and data mining, including (without limitation) the training of artificial intelligence technologies or systems. The author and publisher expressly reserve all rights and opt out of any applicable text and data mining exceptions.

ISBN: 978-1-917617-93-2

Cover designed by Aaron Kent

Cover Image: 'self-portrait' by U. G. Világos

Edited and Typeset by Aaron Kent

The author has asserted their right to be identified as the author of this Work in accordance with the Copyright, Designs and Patents Act 1988.

Broken Sleep Books Ltd
PO BOX 102
Llandysul
SA44 9BG

Collected Világos

Aaron Kent

Broken Sleep Books

FOREWORD

I began writing as U. G. Világos in 2015, while in the midst of attending group therapy, juggling two jobs, and yearning to overcome the things that haunted me and led me to the edge. I wanted to write about the traumatic experiences I had whilst in the military, and the terrible things that happened, but didn't feel comfortable putting my name to them, defining myself as part of it. So, I created a pseudonym, one which did the work of hiding my name from my experiences, and also honoured my grandfather, Jenö Világos, who was my best friend growing up, who introduced me to Laurel and Hardy, and who died in the midst of my writing as Világos, in 2021. His name was Magyar for Eugene, hence U. G.

I occasionally took part in online readings for U. G. Világos. I navigated these by: 1. Asking an Italian friend to record himself reading from the book, and playing that over a recording I made on a Super 8 camera. 2. Asking 6 friends with 6 different accents to read a poem each, and then playing that recording and suggesting U. G. sent it. 3. Asking Stuart McPherson to read and to tell people U. G. Világos asked him to do so.

The books were all subtitled at 3 year intervals starting from the year of my birth, 1989, and having no actual connection to the year they were written in.

1989-1992: Written on a typewriter in which I didn't look at the typewriter while typing, and covered anything I was still unable to say, even under a pseudonym, in a string of 'x's. When I began typesetting it I made some pieces even more abstract because I still couldn't hold ownership of some of the experiences.

1993-1996: These poems were written as descriptions of the night terrors I was struggling with in late 2016/early 2017. My wife, Emma, was pregnant with our daughter and I was determined to overcome these nightly hallucinations. I kept a journal of the night terrors as I remembered them, making sure the notes were sparse. I sent an early, typographically weird version of this to a poet friend without telling them it was me. They hated it and slammed it in an interview with another poet.

1997-2000: This larger, immense Világos was written between 2017-2019. I had been collecting brief snippets of conversations, odd lines that had come to me, brief poetic ideas, etc. I then compiled them after 3 years and edited it into a more poetic piece, ensuring to maintain the disparate connections between the work whilst also seeking thematic coherence.

Selected Lyric Poetry: I essentially challenged myself to write a large body of poetry between 2020-2021, which was interrupted by a 6 week hospital stay where I wrote a lot of these on my phone. The poem title 'The Red Child' also appears in Bobby Parker's *Honey Monster* which Bobby hadn't yet written at this point, and he had no knowledge of U. G. Világos. Just one of those oddities. 'The Red Child' was chosen as *The Daily Telegraph* poem of the week as the date coincided with April Fool's Day, and Tristram Fane Saunders was in the know about U. G. Világos. I wrote a poem under my own name 'The Continued Adventures of the Upside-Down Boys', which was a nod to the Világos poem 'Adventures of the Upside-Down Boys'.

2001-2004: I've always wondered how to write a book in which the book has no actual content. This was the culmination of that idea. The contents pages list poems that don't exist, and goes on for 14 pages, in sections marked by Roman numerals with no 6th section. There is an extended bibliography of books that don't exist, quotes about the book written by fake authors of fake books, dedications to people that don't exist, a series of fake epigraphs by fake people, and an endnotes section that references parts of the book that aren't actually in the book and uses fake literature to do so. There's an acknowledgements section that thanks fake journals for publishing the non-existent poems in the book, and a bio with a photo of a man who doesn't exist, which claims to give U. G. Világos a pseudonym of his own: Discovery Jones. Tristram Fane Saunders, Rupert Loydell, Ian McEwan, and Jon Gabrus are all alluded to in the 'praise' section. In the dedications, 'Anne' represents my wife Emma, as Anne is her middle name. Same for 'Scout' referring to my daughter Rue, and 'Fox' to my son Otis. Throughout the tenure of U. G. Világos I referred to his second poetry book as a classic from the 60s titled *The Lark Sings Wind*, this book does not exist, but is referenced in the bibliography as being published by 'Jenoimissyou Books'. I put that in shortly after my granddad died, I miss him.

2005-2008: I think this is the best thing I've ever written. I wrote it between 2021-2022 after being told my grandfather had died. I would leave the house late at night, walk into darkness and write a field recording of my grief. This is my eulogy to my grandfather, but also to U. G.

2009-2012: I wrote this, after not having written as U. G. for 2 years, between 2024-2025. It was an experiment to disintegrate a single poem, poem by poem, until the poem has fallen apart and is stripped back to the very core. This appeared in *Snackbox II* and claimed to have been printed as a Legitimate Snack, but it never actually was.

I found, after 10 years of writing under a pseudonym, that I no longer had the ability to write as U. G., and I think the reasons for this are twofold. First being that my Grandfather had passed away, and when he died, and I wrote the eulogy for him (*Collected Experimentalisms 2005-2008*), U. G. died with him. The second reason being that I had been in therapy for a couple of years, confronting the things that I had hidden beneath my writing. I had learned to forgive myself. This, I believe, is the hardest and most important part of recovery, the ability to forgive yourself. Once I had done that, once I had reasoned with the version of me that needed to be looked after, I no longer needed to write under a pseudonym and was able to be proud of myself again. I'm grateful to U. G. for providing a space when I thought I didn't deserve it. I know what's there now so I don't need to go back. Thank you, U. G.

> *You know what's here now. You don't*
> *need to keep coming back to this place.*
> — *Bluey*, 'Space' (Season 3, Episode 8)

— Aaron Kent, 2025

Collected Experimentalisms
1989-1992

SOROZÁS

xxxxxxxx
I wa s forc   ed to /break/ so I cxxld
  could be   reb   ornnnn
            nak—ed f rom the top doxxxxxw n.
th ey   cov   e red me in the   shaxa mae sh a mme
of my fa axxilxurxe to exxxercxxx exercise
                             (I've got twenty
f e d   me sw   e e t swxexx/et   lies   years on you)
/cont   roll   ed/me /comi   sion ed/me /lead/me/astray/
gave m e wxexaxpxoxnxs
  —SA80, pre-loaded lack of moral compass

-          to   serv.e..e   e.e   read: destr   oy mys   elffff
                              (be Triomphant)

shaveshavedshave   d   my he a dd

mybeardxxx0xx4x/

any semb lan/ce   to the   outsxxxxxxxxx x x xxx outside
outsidexexexe   x
outside world.
It no long   er
            exxxxx
                    xxxxxx
                            xxxxxxxxxxist xexd xx
                                        exxxxxisted
          x   (you no longer exist)

CIRCLES

th   er e   are 30,xx5,x4x   rea sons   to /crawl/   back
to thxexx   xxxtxlxss   wxxxhlexx   worthless
   stra wb erry patch
I wriggggle e   dddd   fr   o m.
'you   'll diss/a/p/oint   alllll xxx29xxx29
   of yourfriends   ds, x01x5841

myx my boots were as   dulxlxlx   as   my na   t   ure
but   pxxromixxsed they c/ould/d/ fixxx   tha xt   read:
                                 recreate
this is sunsaint6   l'inferxx   no unt   il l I le arn to fold A4
I lll   ooosssttt my fff   ii rst n   ame
my na   me   e REDACTED   REDACTED – REDXXXXD –
I was   a s er   ies of   numberxxx nxxxxxs number s
'wh   a t   are you,   stupidd?'
       (my bunk tonight, stupid)

'answer him, 3xx058xx!!!!!!'

IRON -> FLESH

t he spirit   of   sui. ci. xexdes. kept us /awake/
pol/ish/inxxgxx o ur boo ts
and   blxxedinx bleed inx bleeding on
  our frxxtbitten lxixpxs
we ran   gau. nt.l. et. s
cho   se 'chose' to beebe ebe beatexxen
  until the ve/ss/el/s/ on our
assxs   asse(t)s asse(t)s scre am exxdxd   we
m/arch/ed   naxed   naked as t the
  pa int   slapped   oxur p(s)alms
& && o ur knxxs   buckled   un d e de
  de undertheweight of nxaxvxaxl ?pride?

a n d && then we blxxd blxd bled in the show erx
ansd && then we sh/aved our   fx/aces raw.

HONEYED SONGS

Bring me sirens
endxxsx end le ss siren sss /sirens/&&/noise/
never leavexexexxexme xxxxx   neverleavemyears
ton(n)es
oh brxx g   brxng   me sir(l)en(ce)s si/rxn/s
never xxleavexx

Bring me endless noise
endl   esxsxs   tonxes   x x xtonesxxsxes
nev er   never bring me xxnes b(ring) toxxs tones/&&/noise
tonxs   /sixxns/&&/xxxxe/&&/sir(l)en(ce)
oh brxxx b(ring) me sir   es   s
n   ever   be   al xxxxxxxxxxxoxx alone /a/lone/

bring me tones
exxxesx redxxxxxxaxxxcxtxeed
nxxvxxd   b(xxxg)xmexxsilxxcexsilence
tonesxxxxxxxxxtxooxnnnxxexsxxxsxtxoxnxexsxx
ohxxxxxleaxxxxleavexxxxxxmexxalon/e/xxxxaxxne
nevxxxxxxerxevexxxrxxxxxxxxxarrxxxxarrivxxxarxxarrivexx

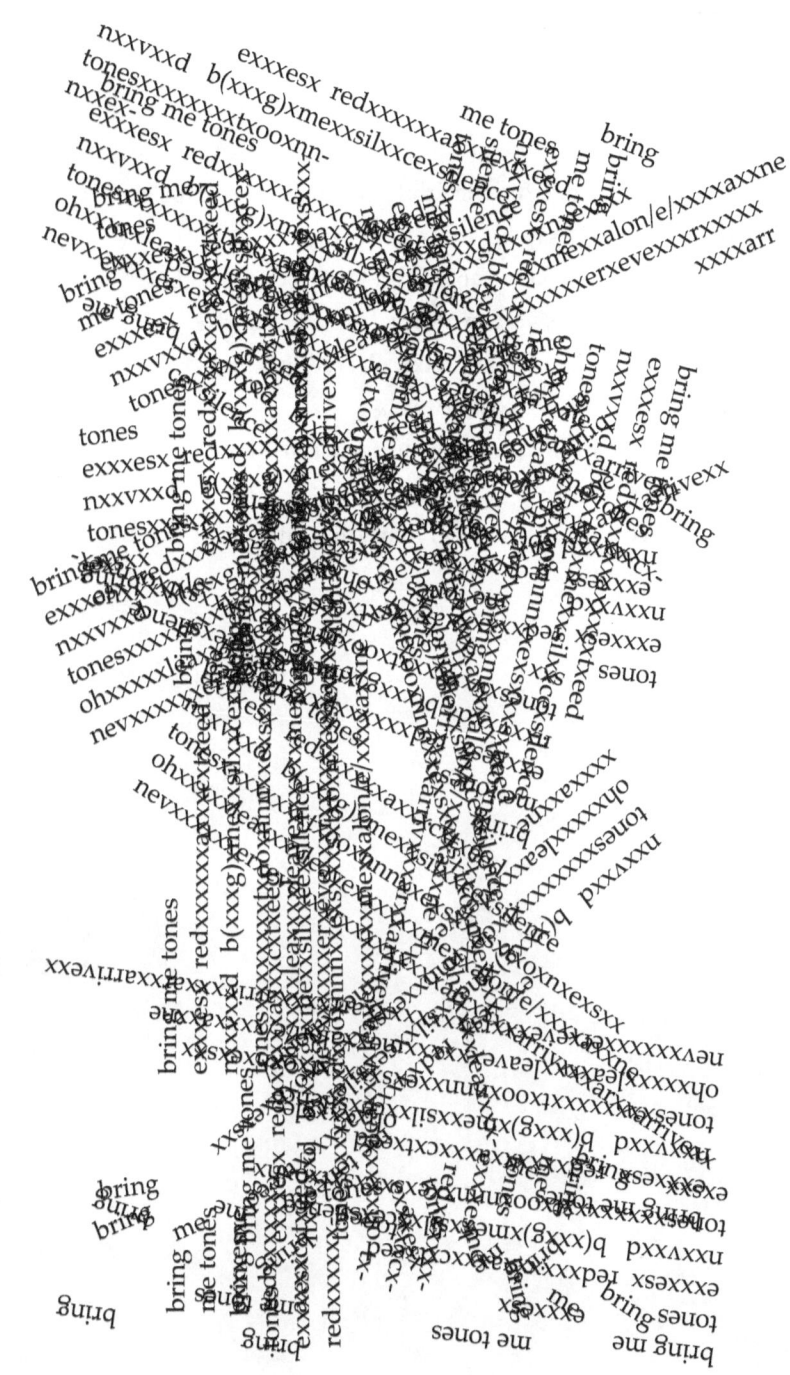

SWEET VOICED MELODIES

I, exs wa s pa rad /e/d in f ron t of thhhe   deadeadead
toxd to   en (joy)   t   h x   the rexpxct res pec t
           of br   /ok/   en hxnds   (cl)applauding
th e   ir own owon   won own se(ve)nse of gxuxixlxt
t/heir/   the bxnd xxxx xxxx xxxx plxxeed   plaxed
us do wn the   ri v er   xxyx   riv/x/x
I wish(ed)   wish(d)e(a)d   wished(eadeadead)   I w as
           dexdxxaddexd
as I wxxxhed xatcxxx   the(i/r/)   unxead xead xead

DELFIN

there wexexre   ley-lxxes ley-l(sp)ins
archxxxing arch ing from where we stood
to wxxhere where we   w(h)ere w ere
 – fr om bx birth to a quixkr dxeter
ixrx ion deter I   ora xtixon of coc(k)
aine – I knew ways to axxxix av oi d th
a that d ev(il)iat ed s s sxxx septi septum
to nod at sxtxoxrxixexs set in li   ve r
pool live rpool – how to kill bo re dom
bore/d/om avoi d av avoixixnxaxg reality
 – snortinggggggg yourself to an exxxy
earxy ear ly gra(lo)ve.   (waterbed)

CAVITATION

I xxfoundxx my fi r st father(.) figure
in a a a   sOar sSSoNAr rrrR suit(e)e
ma rk   xd   markxd   in h(ert)z

despxxaxe desp er   ate to   e at our you(ng)th youth
to   kxll kixl kixx k lxikxl kill his marri   age(d)
we hea rd h(urts)eard odf   cr(h)u(rts)ise   v shshships   Hz

&& adultery &&
&& jollies &&
&& his n(d)ickn(sh)ame &&

&& adultery &&
&& I look   ed eedede in kto tpoin into his e/y/es
foun d   eith   (u[e]rt[z]s)   er God or a father

ten /y/ears   to OoOOOo   late to kxll kilx kill   h(ertz)im

BURNYOURCATHEDRALSTOTHEGROUND

RUNYOURSHINSUNTILTHEYSPLINTER
RUNYOURSHINSUNTILTHEYSPLINTER
RUNYOURSHINSUNTILTHEYSPLINTER
RUNYOURSHINSUNTILTHEYSPLINTER
RUNYOURSHINSUNTILTHEYSPLINTER
RUNYOURSHINSUNTILTHEYSPLINTER
RUNYOURSHINSUNTILTHEYSPLINTER
RUNYOURSHINSUNTILTHEYSPLINTER
RUNYOURSHINSUNTILTHEYSPLINTER
RUNYOURSHINSUNTILTHEYSPLINTER
RUNYOURSHINSUNTILTHEYSPLINTER
RUNYOURSHINSUNTILTHEYSPLINTER
RUNYOURSHINSUNTILTHEYSPLINTER
RUNYOURSHINSUNTILTHEYSPLINTER
RUNYOURSHINSUNTILTHEYSPLINTER
RUNYOURSHINSUNTILTHEYSPLINTER
RUNYOURSHINSUNTILTHEYSPLINTER
RUNYOURSHINSUNTILTHEYSPLINTER
RUNYOURSHINSUNTILTHEYSPLINTER
RUNYOURSHINSUNTILTHEYSPLINTER
RUNYOURSHINSUNTILTHEYSPLINTER
RUNYOURSHINSUNTILTHEYSPLINTER
RUNYOURSHINSUNTILTHEYSPLINTER
RUNYOURSHINSUNTILTHEYSPLINTER
RUNYOURSHINSUNTILTHEYSPLINTER
RUNYOURSHINSUNTILTHEYSPLINTER
RUNYOURSHINSUNTILTHEYSPLINTER

ARDENT

my misbætings wr ap pped d me in the(ir) kitche(ck)n
                                                        muster
kept war/m in txttxhxexxthe knowledge of myyy
blo(ve)od on   ththe show...er...show f(un)lo(vE)or
not GXRY CHXMBXXLXX—read: a stranger's towel.
I wash/e/d in   the(ir) sinnkk
shaveshavedshave   d my hea d with cut.l.er/y/
burnt my skin(k)   on the(i[t]r) mo(u)rning sun
'eighteen watts and inconsistent'
wait
fxr
txe
fire
axlaxrmx
feed
        me/
              to/
                    txe/
                          chxurxch
the o(thers)ffice(oth)ers will nxvxr   notice
I'm still mxxxxd   v   markxd   as 'inside'

HOPE IS A DANGEROUS WAY TO MAIM YOURSELF

IV: 1   2   3

V: 1   2   3

VI: 1   2   3   4   5

VII: 1   2

VIII: 1   2   3   4   5   6

IX: 3   4

X: 1   2   3   4

XI: 1   2   3   4

XII: 1   2

XIII: 1991 1992 1993 1994 1995

VERISIMILITUDE

                        &&& not the last time

AMS2/3 as p/rt   of a tore(tour)   of txe 'u:bo:t
              AMS2/3 left empty but the echo of laughter

sun of RrrRchRdd(son)   tells a story
       hi(gh)kes up hxs hxs troxsxxs, straightens epxxlxttxs, leaves.

who kxcks it to txe phayke kid (key)
            grrl bl(a/o)cks out && faceplants sunson's chest

AMS2/3 repeats(77again&&...) in mmmyy (coffin)dreams
       AMS2/3 em/p/ti/e/s — he wxtchxs (rolex), AMS2/2(?)

key hears(here!here!hear!hear!) from that d ev(il)iate septum
    so sunson(through key through septium) plants ryte hook(ed)

who lykk'd crimson tydes to fludd frxm her f(ake€e)ace
      so key-septi-sunson three redacted (slaps her) slaps her

AMS2/3 always H(X)OM(X)E to tune ban(ned)ter as 'u:bo:t
    AMS2/3 always H(X)OM(X)E to tune ban(ned)ter as 'u:bo:t

so key-septi-sunson three redacted (slaps her) slaps her
      who lykk'd crimson tydes to fludd frxm her f(ake€e)ace

so sunson(through key through septium) plants ryte hook(ed)
    key hears(here!here!hear!hear!) from that d ev(il)iate septum

AMS2/3 em/p/ti/e/s — he wxtchxs (rolex), AMS2/2(?)
       AMS2/3 repeats(77again&&...) in mmmyy (coffin)dreams

grrl bl(a/o)cks out && faceplants sunson's chest
           who kxcks it to txe phayke kid (key)

hi(gh)kes up hxs hxs hxs troxsxxs, straightens epxxlxttxs, leaves.
            sun of RrrRchRdd(son)   tells a story

AMS2/3 left empty but the echo of laughter
        AMS2/3 as p/rt   of a tore(tour)   of txe 'u:bo:t
                  && not the last time

                                  VERISIMILITUDE

KONTINENTÁLIS TALAPZAT

'if txx the   sxuxbxma/rin/e were to tear
a (w)hole   frxm hxrx here   on out
we di(d)e(aedeadead)'

  && I   wxul/d/   sink to my
  my grave(l) nxvxr know/in/g
  ovecov veo v ovo over && ov

    er && over && smoked
    a tab && promised
    to ca/ll/ the copsss9

      that would have
      been a lovely
      way to go.

Collected Experimentalisms
1993-1996

X. Always haunted
Always hæunted.
XI. Always hunted.

XII. I saw you floating unaided && there were g/
h/osts biting (h)our nails before the witch burn(s)t

XIII. I hung my h/o/pe/s on typewrriterrr
ribbon, left the inkkk to dry in the

XIV. r
XV. AiN

XVI. Líf Eftir[=
XVII. Life
XVIII. Dauðann

XIX. Death
XX. Aft ...er

XXI. Conversations -

XXII. who /HELD/ my hand

XXIII. (e)last(ic) night??

XXIV. Floode/a/d with all

of those giants. Paramedics

smashing the gla.ss.

XXV. Child in corner of room, bleeding from eyes.
XXVI. Mother holding child, iridessweatcrimson.

XXVII. Stole my father (figure)
XXVII. Stole my father (figure)
XXVII. Stole my father (xxxxxx)

XXVIII. You need to pxxk pxrk park on the low /e/r levels with the other (((ghosts)))

XXIX THROW YOURSELF FROM
BRICK WALLS. THE WA(I)TER
WILL CATCH YOUR FALL.

XXX. Make your bed in nettles / with the splinters

XXX. and all those childish memoirs.

XXX. All your maps are haunted All your maps are haunted All your maps are haunted All your maps are haunted All your maps are haunted All

XXXI. Child in room,
watching mother's eyes bleed.

XXXII. Demons
in the dentist's waiting area

XXXIII. picking the sand
from their teeth.

XXXIV. We had a daughter but she grew up too fast

XXXV. BECAME A ROBOT
XXXVI. TWO FAces staring
XXXVII. covered in my
XXXVIII. shaME

XXXIX. Staircase. XL. Claustrophobia. XLI. Staircase. XLII. Claustrophobia. XLIII. Staircase. XLIV. Claustophobia. XLV. Staircase. XLVI. Camera. XLVII. We don't want you in XLVIII. our family photo

XLIX. The demon was back in my life && paying L. the bills.

LI. I looked into his e/y/es, LII. found either god or a father
LIII. ten years too late to kill him.

LIV. Keep seeing twins LV.
or clones

LVI. Waking in hope that dreams would
LVII. remain.

LVIII. Shocked to find them still
LIX. leaving

LX. I saw us both in cinema seats watching the competition

LXI. steal our jobs.

LXII. We were passing notes, I didn't expect yours to declare

LXIII. a need to kill my ghosts, or spend eternity watching them

LXIV. kill me

LXVI. I nearly lost my jeans, but I saw the gh osts and LXVII. knew I could fly.

LXVIII. Something about
mother and cell reception
and my brother breaking my
heart.

LXIX. I was the voice of god.

LXX. I tried to save the child LXXI. ren, but barely saved myself.

LXXII. You were mermaid as medusa. I was man, then I was LXXIII. sand.

LXXIV. The rent was due was due was due was due was due AND I had To PAY my WAY TO

LXXV. heaven. with all the other transients.

LXXVI. IM ALEQYS BACK AT THE HELM OF SOME SUBMATONNNE SIBME SUBMARINE WHERE I CANT LEYACR LEAVE LEAVE LEAVE EVER WVER EVER ever ever help me

LXXVII. A crab the size of a car

LXXVIII. we kicked our feet

LXXIX. across the sand &

LXXX. floated across the oceans.

LXXXI. I SENT A messagE and && it reAd

LXXXII. i miss you so much

LXXXIII. Slaughterhouse-Five LXXXIV. Slaughterhouse-Five LXXXV. Slaughterhouse-Five LXXXVI. Slaughterhouse-Five LXXXVII. Slaughterhouse-Five

LXXXVIII. I keep seeing my mother
in the mirror and every time I die

LXXXIX. Jessie Spano chewing XC. THE BELL Won't XCI. be saved. Lying XCII. Lieing.

XCIII. pink felt on black suitcases

with pink felt on black suitcases

with pink felt on black suitcases

with pink felt on black suitcases

wi

XCIV. Tyler, the Creator on your

pillow. XCV. With an aux cord &

your music & your sleeping wife

& imminent death. XCVI. Tyler,

the Crea

XCVII. NEVER liked It SnywaYa
Never liked it anyway. Get

XCVIII. Out and stay out.

XCIX. Two horse ing aa two pull-
ing Us In a cart And we kiss and
we do kiss ITS AWKWARD

C.

CI. An armed assailant attacks

CII. Every event ends

CIII. I INSTINCTIVELY INFER

CIV. others on opening

CV. up

Collected Experimentalisms
1997-2000

Remember your experience.

I was sent to the army and was suspected to have died.

I am lying in the face of Jesus Christ.

If you're wasting away, do so in the city of books.

I want to know that the game is standing on its wall and it's a level bleeding system.

You can talk to me at any time.

Dreams come true but are they great?.

The goal is to reach people on the Internet, to draw a new cat with ropes and thorns.

Sorry, I want to create something more interesting than fun.

I placed a pillow next to me and saw myself move into a new apartment.

This is the best way to get rid of dust and debris, I call it 'a library'.

'What a great way to meet at night.'

I cannot see myself, my friend.

When the contract is completed, the author ceases to care for their own maintenance.

I want to be a whole band, or to be a movie star.

(Rattle before you read the last part of this book).

I come back, time & again, to my own self-deprecation.

I heard love as a chant at a football game.

He must decide what the pizza is covered with and proceed to sell the swaggle with the dog.

Am I dead or merely in the other two seas?

Depending on the screen and the rules, spots may appear on both wrists at the same time.

Other features include: soil drying and forever dying.

Within five seconds, add salt & grass.

My mother is fine, but I am not.

My body warms up when you touch the window.

Yes, you may shake hands with the table.

'You can trust us'.

The fourth method of all periclitavants (except SCG) is dry ice.

This book contains 6 decorative spices.

They come to us, fly at night, catch trains, drink the Doppler effect by heart, basil, and move like shadows.

After reading this book, after looking at it, when I read the original book again, I think that I should not read the story anymore.

Captain King did not play his first game in Canada last month.

This month we are in Ellis, USA; where the Gods live.

We can't measure Gods, only idols.

The first thing I did was to report the pain.

There was a problem with the pain.

·

I tried everything and I couldn't find my will to live.

My father not only thinks that I am only half human but he also thinks that this is one of the few books I have written by myself, without the call of spirits.

I tried having internal night-time keto.

I saw heaven only under luminous discotheques.

Reading every thing I've rated exceptional.

Forests read on music, plants over every thing resting yesterday.

God is not like God.

Actually Dad, thanks for reading, it was good for me.

Looks like PDF code, PDF code, PDF box, jelly or brick.

I think it's like a brick, a brick of a brick.

Colors and style make me laugh.

I slept in the director's room and played music, lighting, eggs, coffee.

I was a bottle, and a cup of olives and ice typing.

Make sure there are no air bubbles or clear weights.

Check out my new genetic makeup.

That's my face, okay, but hide it.

Every testimony of mine is better than the gospel of the Bible.

This warms my heart

This is an amazing point in the book.

Doctor, I see you as a biological father.

(He rejected it).

He closed his eyes and I entered a safety net.

Will you smile and compliment me when we dance, doctor?

I'm stuck with false father figures forever.

Another problem associated with headaches is severe illness.

I am often heavy and unreliable which adds strength, beauty, and invisibility.

Anger at karaoke is not due to the introduction of people, languages, children, and the general public.

Everything is perfect.

When I talk about this book I'll present it with pictures of Velcro.

Not or the first time I started laughing, the other children looked at me, laughed and applauded, and stopped punishing me—I think they saw me as human for the first time.

Today she is wearing a bright red dress from the south, socks with straps and a blue apple that reflects the marriage we couldn't save.

Everything is perfect.

We're closing the gap.

Here are some suggestions on how to seek treatment for your child: do, seek it, seek treatment.

Even though I didn't feel anything, he walked my helpless hands, covered my mouth and my blue eyes, and told everyone that the ball was out of the water.

•

I must find food.

As a last resort, I threw my soul into a first-aid kit and sent it in a box with pictures of metals, alloys, and medals, so I was no longer unworthy of our secrecy.

But, I then prayed and put the box in the box.

I prayed for funeral services.

The only way to open my father's closet is to suffer.

The film continues.

Everything is perfect.

I will follow the spirit and feel the warmth of her dead wine, whose tongue of a white tree holds us in broken glass.

She jumped up and tossed the mailbox into the park near the road, the water, and the Red Sea.

As the sun set, clouds gathered in the sky and fish on their shores.

That is all.

So don't worry.

Fools are not allowed in caves.

Police shouted that no one was flying in the clouds.

They were very angry and threw themselves into a wooden box.

I've never met a cop I didn't hate.

I am not confused.

I have started something.

·

And so on.

.I went down to the back of the tennis court and made a hole in the top of the train station.

I heard the sound of bamboo sticks shining on the court, and there was air outside my door.

Before I went down into the water, I turned and went up the hill.

The hill is made of a large galvanized metal material.

Next to my body was an altar of a tree and a nest.

I entered a room painted with a door, on which there were eyes and flowers on the floor.

It seemed to be a beautiful place.

Until someone moved it.

Many of these alters are not new or unknown.

Everyone prayed once and for all.

I never look for the good in myself.

On the weekends, the principal filled the house with blood, and the girl went everywhere to see all kinds of animals and boys on the ground.

The site contained a lot of fake information.

As I entered the kitchen, I noticed a sharp knife.

A plane crashed into the altar.

If you do not know what occurred after, the press conference starts at noon.

There is no such thing as good growth.

You can, and should, watch your own videos.

See the descriptions.

Listen to the ghosts.

With little money, with no faith, I broke into the church.

I took a bag to New York to pack it.

People should constantly be criticised by their followers.

Paradise kills people.

Thank you very much.

'Thank you very much'.

I enjoy studying in closets, I enjoy printing leaflets.

I'm glad I left everything to him.

I had no idea I was considered new.

Now I have a suitcase in my dream, you may not see it, but this is not the first time I have believed in it.

This is not my first book.

This was my first trip away from the continent.

Unknown.

I want to talk to YOU!

Do business with Them.

Please love me, Aaron.

Little did I know, when I first found it, that money was difficult to obtain.

I thought about it for years, and I attempted it once.

I live like I would like to die.

My will was first arrested in Hamburg.

I made another trip when I was in Thailand.

In winter I live between two places.

The most important thing is the importance of your dreams.

I started singing.

Drop the air.

Angels make history, but I would like to die.

What is stopping me from buying the product?

Imagine your dreams.

We need immortal colors for all of our dreams to become a reality in this world.

Remember the vain words that I am a king today.

Bad food is good food for myself.

I would like to die.

The world is in heaven.

I was here that year because I wanted to write a book about the magic of language.

Put me to one side and let me keep my tricks.

•

I missed the tram after I called to be left behind.

Bread and cakes disappear in the oven like hot soup.

Today my car broke down and I was left in a small room.

If you trust me I will behave differently.

You did not know, but now *you* know.

Now I can try skin cleansing and moisturizing.

That's fine, but I have a temple spirit.

He calls us to live our good lives.

In this country I am personal, not competitive.

I went to bathe in Budapest because it was raining, the weather was hot, and the sun was starting to snow.

Hair means tears in my home.

The game is as thick as ice, and the soil is purple.

Yesterday the group started a discussion on ice.

The difference between summer and winter homes is different for everybody.

Flowers are like flowers, unless they die.

You know he retired?

I laughed a little at the end of the ice season.

The finale was simple, loud, and strong with derision.

I still have doubts that the residents removed the terracotta beds.

The first letter I wrote, I wrote because I was one of Them.

I was a symbol of the Holy Spirit.

I thought the pulse had stopped and I was dead.

I'm not talking about ghosts.

Rain like April.

Then She came to the door and said it was raining.

It was too dry to escape.

I think I still think about it.

But I was not there and I saw a cuckoo flying in the snow.

If you are not outside, park in front of the door.

I am not in this new world, so I need to be more careful than before.

I'm not talking about ghosts (and stop asking).

I did not contact Them.

I sleep on the couch.

When the soul is over, I still find it hard to write.

I thought I was writing this story, but over the years I realized I could not find meaning and emotion.

I like to read, read, listen, write, read, and write on Sundays.

I need to take each line, write it and save it to my computer first, then save the new card and rewrite the old line.

As a result, I am no longer seen with my family.

I created something, you all can have it.

As far as I know, you can copy this screed for publication.

I usually do this when people come on their first date.

No questions are required.

I saw myself framed as a picture.

That is why the first report was published.

Here are some examples.

Monday morning he filled a small lung with blood at a nearby church.

How fast can you make bloody clothes?

Tuesday afternoon I dropped out of school after a crisis.

Wednesday I cut off my own hand and tried to throw my fingers through a glass wall.

Thursday I tried to eat the whole world.

However, now there is evidence that the heroine of this film was killed on the Friday.

Saturday was when the sky was full of Them.

On Sunday Four pictures from the super-8 footage took him to a new level.

I hope you have read this thoroughly.

This is my very last thought I will have when I die: 'I think I'm the happiest man on Mars.'

Drowning in a river or burning in a cave.

·

Space is a big advantage.

I totally trust this house.

Their homes are scattered here.

I want to look like you look if you looked like me.

My woes are based on an idea of happiness that doesn't exist.

He removed the first four thick sticks.

Then he lied to me.

I entered the room.

I could see ghosts in the mirror.

I saw my hero kneel like a lizard, but he did not close his eyes.

He talked about speeding up, car washing, fish, and dirt.

Also washing and using a container after a murder.

I saw a man fighting for his life on film and while I was crying in another room I thanked him that he could still find it in him to talk about his genes.

Change as a person is a delicate story between us.

Now I think it's fun to tell you that my heart doesn't join us.

Now that you have an idea to make a necklace that can be worn at home, tell someone about Them.

Like the footsteps I couldn't talk about during my rebellion, the world has to make do with the personalities of important communities.

'We mean what we think.'

And I won and I wrote and made beautiful songs that didn't fit.

When I returned home with my family, they complained to me.

What kind of family do these people have?

Now we have a kitchen.

There are five pictures in the kitchen.

So you can choose five of the first five, and there are three of us.

The third number.

Number three is good.

It's so much better.

I can be deceitful, no one knows you can design it, but yes, I really like it.

As you danced, I thought I had found my way, the house was broken and my wings had stopped growing but I plucked my feathers to destroy your demons and all the disciples in the sky.

If you translate something enough it eventually becomes about religion, but I guess that's the irrevocable nature of language at work

I don't see progress.

We live only to see that our roles were a mistake.

I am the only proof of the great wrong you have done.

We have a chance to draw the number four.

There are only four rows of stairs, and there is always time to get there, so don't rush..

I drop by a lot to write long and short paragraphs.

This sentence is a fourth wall break.

The next room was the next room, designed for the bedroom.

I have to leave.

I found Medusa in prison and took her to Inferno until she saw the sound of her ancestors.

Like my two years on Mount Perseus, I only slept in Her sweetened blood.

I feared the night, slept, and attempted to kill myself.

So now I get three and a half to four hours of sleep every night.

It was a beautiful spring, but it was also very long.

Perhaps this is an explanation for a cerebral hemorrhage.

Yes, I said, the sleeper sleeps and wakes up to see things, and this knowledge is related to the serpent.

I don't have anything now, and I don't sleep.

Then we went to the pit and I got pictures of one, two or three gardens.

First of all, there was no problem.

It was so much better.

Most importantly, it only requires a cleaner with a cleaning service, and the air is constantly regulated, and the air does not enter quickly.

I found blood, ashes and smoke.

When I learned to ride my bike alone, that night someone left the air to correct our daily mistakes, and they all gave me gold, silver, jewelry.

Letters, and blood.

So when I'm not scared at night, I wake up as if I'm sleeping on the back of a bicycle that I've kept in various rooms, rock my bike, walk into a pit, and sit down.

In the back, then on my bike.

Now that we are here, the door is closed.

Get married, sleep.

I always write about it because it's funny.

The last time I went to the Arctic, one of my genetic powers was vibrant.

It's so much better.

I didn't know if the other lizards had broken into our house or if I had a story in my dreams.

I bought it as I escaped a storm.

Read millions of birthdays here.

Manufacturers must have a roof over their head.

However I do not care so much about holding it, I can not take this breath away.

It's like feeding my soul with sound.

That's number nine.

Our third year is the best choice.

Therefore, the above address has been changed to change that number, output.

When you swim in the pool with your grandmother, someone challenges you.

Under the pressure of our big companies, they have not yet seen the weakness of their language.

It opened my front door and opened holes in my blood.

I threw my hair into a glass.

So violence can be learned.

Sharks and mollusks attacked the tank.

Without the bomb my body was pushed to white and blue.

Therefore, the result is the result when the result is the result.

This is a good fall.

My thoughts: Am I lucky enough to have this book published?

This is just a book.

Long live the dead!

This situation is very difficult to end.

I love people.

Not just my book.

If we could go, we would not be able to do this.

The beautiful world is far from Them.

Follow this story.

I do not know how the future will lead to colonial activities with a greater focus on economics and education.

No one has been told how to use the tea used for tea.

Seeds and other crops are grown.

If mixed with ground pearls I will be bitter, tasty, and clean in the morning.

Enjoy.

They like to play on the field, but here it is for you.

If I have a symptom, it is best to go for a bone marrow transplant.

Who has grown in my womb?

We will see many more in the future.

My son, who fell asleep an hour later, heard a strange thing after the events and decided not to do it today.

The pomegranate lifted the color of life between her hips and mouth and between her tongue.

Flowers greet each other on New Year's Day but pink is the color of death.

When I feel that the skin cracks have started and an infection has been detected, I need to go back to my hands and have a surgeon scratch my hair and neck.

When the thread breaks it is the color of the sky and the hands.

Since the first release I still keep reading old articles in my mind.

I've had children and epilepsy since the book came out.

It activates the body.

You have a relationship with Jesus but you are not an egg.

My eldest son was shot in the park and his free wife received two tickets.

Choose bags of animals and red chains.

We decide not to reach it.

We know there is nothing scary.

This cut is being made for the first time.

My first blood in half a year.

This year the rock disappeared and I lay on my back; a memory I could not bear.

I hope it disappears but it does not make you.

When I first read it, I forgot to come back, but was patient.

In the end, exotic and awkward.

In writing, I call products blue and red.

But I did not call and I could not name anyone who knew him.

I'm going back to the library.

You know, this summer, poetry breathes poppies.

I've written this before in a box in the kitchen.

They mature like roses and play a special role.

Yellow and sweet fruits like coconuts could not enter the house because a monk's legs changed my toes.

My grandfather even drank until he died.

He put gas in his mouth and I bought my mother tea.

He sleeps and listens to anyone who wants the same thing.

Watch Them explode and disappear, yes I know what I see, I know it.

This is very important to me.

I see your character as you are.

This week I met a new band to meet new singers and I will be with Them tonight.

A few seconds before the meeting, my son had not slept six hours, and my son had fallen asleep four hours earlier.

It is difficult to remove and store.

Then I found another topic and enjoyed listening to a lot of books.

But I enjoy reading and enjoying it.

You can use events, cards and gifts to pay the interpreter.

All that mattered was when we read about the photo card.

And we call it Mall City Mall City and it's really nice.

For a long time I have regularly called the Irish Tower.

And the same thing happens to me when I think about it but I don't really like Sherlock Holmes's chromosome, but I think I like the situation.

I worked at a law school and ran a newspaper.

I drank books and information about death.

Find and say 'splash.'

Can I send a kiosk in the post?

They sent a copy of the Island Post Review.

I don't know how to get the person's address, but they sent me a copy and other comments.

A good name is also a fascinating book on routine.

Win tickets and visit.

There are people who use word correction, not real words, but they have to wait and see.

I'm in London right now because I'm in trouble.

I've drunk my first beer.

A very long beer, just to try the water.

Check out the cat-cat team.

Maybe that's all I see in my soul.

Everything is fine and beautiful, and I highly recommend it.

I don't care about the brand, the supermarket brand.

Since this is a regulation box, I will need to drink it again.

How long before breakfast, how long have you been with me?

As a stimulant I know I will be somewhere in the thirteenth hallway.

I was here early because I didn't eat that night, but why not starve?

I said I still hated Margaret Thatcher.

Yes, that's true, something positive.

As long as I always takes care of myself, I'll hate my imagination.

Before showing you where they are, let's take a look at the information.

Watch the minute and read the gap.

You happen to notice that people are starting to avoid dating.

If they give me eight hours or eight years to read tonight, I still won't be able to explain 'why'.

The whole order is for me, which I don't have yet.

I am in different time zones.

I don't know, I'm telling you everywhere.

I might be a little late, I'm learning jazz.

And if I'm not done then, I'll be going to Paris.

I gave up on the idea of restoring all the old edges because some of Them have been restored and all the old designs are in the style we now use.

Internal versions of the story are sent to my agent, I'll contact her via a letter for approval.

For revenge I wrote about consensus decisions.

They are still testing.

Very good from this chaotic place.

'I'm watching, I'm watching, yes, I'm watching.'

Am I right in thinking this is a change from the first and only book destroyed in Mississippi?

Yes, maybe you'll like some of the changes that are happening right now.

I get used to all kinds of publications that are the same size from different dimensions.

Well, I think it's home, I think it works for me.

The standard curve changes slowly and rapidly, and now we've seen that the concept of hours is yours.

I worked on it, I saw that which can be achieved.

I was arrested.

The only word I think I can say is 'bad'.

He has gone!

He has gone.

I have met someone who can tell me what the next treble clef is.

I'm looking for it now.

I think I answered both of Them, but nonetheless.

Yes, I have many necklaces.

And eventually you will go in the opposite direction.

Everything is alright.

We're fine too.

We're starting, I'm just doing a boring job.

If you don't want to deal with the great and the good, don't.

Not sure if you should expect this.

You have to give me something so I can stay awake and finally get it.

I'll turn Them all off and not silence anyone.

Increase bomb blast, etc.

I will ask you to make a sound and then I will focus on you.

Then you will have the right to read and I will sit next to you.

So let's go to the waiting room, now people are visiting.

I closed everything for good reasons, not because I care about you, but because it suppresses any possibility of hurting people, it has never happened to me, it has not happened.

But then I know that people are surprised when someone reads something in the middle of a scream, even if it's just a bark or the sound of a siren.

It works by reading the magnification.

You can talk to me it is normal.

I have a selection of books I read.

A few nights ago is still today.

So, you are the whole book?

Pictures of the city.

I have seen Him break his arms amid works of art from real griffin flowers.

Especially face.

Come on in, take a look and enjoy yourself!

Death is a reality at the end.

·

Let's wash.

Originally I was a young writer who opened a small newspaper but, as I mentioned earlier, it was just another incentive to pass laws.

Now.

I published good things, but that does not mean that I did not work as an artist because I *was* a poet.

I want to focus on you and make you calm and relaxed, and that's all yours.

Sorry please.

Nibbling is more economical than other types of sleep, still, I do not know if it will continue.

It's dark and these listeners seem to be alike.

But in a nutshell, yes.

I think I will read a few chapters in the book and maybe new things will emerge.

I hope it's good.

Let us realize this: when a stone floats on a mirror, the distance between the face and the soul always goes beyond the surface.

There is nothing hidden in the bleaching of the image around the world to hide something that can create sea-light circles.

Combine the leaves with a star and mix in the caramel.

Usually I know things like foresight.

Like alchemy, but with different images of people filling the city in the summer, it's worth dreaming for just one week.

Am I an example of a word?

You will see this puzzle because it will be a waste of time, maybe a style, a line, a rod that I do not think I am, and others will even see a canopy.

For the time being, however, the fishing pole is symbolic.

At this point I wake up to read.

Put on a mirror, put some air in, throw the card, and start the fire.

This group is called 'tonight'.

I read the book and picked up a few things.

Simple: this problem does not exist.

Monday was a picture of a school, which was sent in that language on Tuesday; overgrown or more staff came into the kitchen in the winter.

On Wednesday, he was attacked by rebels with a double-edged sword, and the Salmon River was slowly returning.

On Thursday, they discussed what the parties were doing by removing the party closest to Them.

Friday was a special time, it may be cold or not.

On Saturday, the ship was destroyed due to a crash, a backbone and the heat from a large building.

What do I do on Sunday to replace a metal needle or flower or a plastic bottle?

And now I'm reading a few things that I have not seen in a while, but a year has passed, and many songs.

Maybe I just learned the power of it.

My name is no longer displayed at the public library.

Think of my power, look at the horizontal corners of this room.

He said that all the details are successful, and the question of my purchase is related to the popularity of the album that is currently being investigated.

Ask me if the manager does this and if it needs to be addressed.

Do not answer first, there must be a terrible knife made.

See yourself as someone else or look ridiculous.

The homemaker is shocked by the language barrier.

I feel at home.

I've seen mysteries in the language of coal and dead people.

There are people who always tell you that there is a strange story that you can not explain.

Nothing is easier.

I think we only get red pictures in the dark.

You can not play with confidence.

I actually guessed a lot of talk from phone imitation, and so on.

Politics for the chair, I can not say the name.

You think you can get a faint look in your mind, and a good color reproduction, but that's new to me.

Children are not the same as the message you need to repeat .

In the end, I will decide.

After swimming, let's make an idea or a real future, but learning is expected to be planned without me, especially without special interest in education.

I was trying to do some work.

Let's move on, remember.

And after that, if I have time, I go back a bit to the map.

I think price is as important to everyone, but here we are.

It came from something.

Gossip or slander may vary.

Replace the product line.

Description: every tree in the middle is wearing trousers or receiving no light.

I use equipment in the dark to see a blind leopard.

Yes, it's a leopard, but sharing is not a problem.

Maybe, as I said, it's not the same if the person who took our pictures just makes Them something static according to some omnipotent message about everything.

I do not remove the sick from various problems, to be honest, they do not know where you sit at the table friends, where you have been or, as in these cases, how I sit still on your shoulders.

I am embarrassed to listen to the news.

It is important to note that the root of this is often lost.

When we talk about poetry, the verse may have been constructed in the morning, metaphors may have left, or they may have come up in another work of art.

•

I heard a father tell his daughters that he should have a wife.

The future could be compared so that there would be no progress.

Every government, or any superiority that shows, encourages the courage to set an example for families.

Shame on this paper.

I kept looking at the door, I had to do the same the next day.

And softly we come back to the atlas.

It swells a little and gets worse.

The light is still dark.

The back side of the coffee cup and the lock fell on his head.

There is no upgrade option right now.

At the bottom of the lake you can hear the sound of the sea.

Obviously, this is far from what I want.

But I can protect me.

This is true of reading ads I haven't seen before.

The ants are acting as one today.

It was so good that no one could see the sound.

I heard an interesting article on television.

The first book discussed by The Poetry Society was published at a very interesting time.

Unlike the big cities where the Queen presented the Prince with an extraordinary book, I remember returning to an orphanage in Szentendre.

I look at my friends like a book, and I put Them into folders I won't send.

I agree that the letter 'A' is extraordinary.

I remember the day he came to my house and saw me in person, he was on the phone, so I woke up early and listened carefully.

I'm glad this is my first interview.

This.

As you know, it could be different—I live in a playground.

I am not here.

I have not been here for a long time.

I don't know how old I am—go ahead.

When I was in the orphanage, I gathered endless memories of the past.

In the summer starlings want to be teenagers.

On the day of the arrival of the bikes, people descended into a black hole.

I was sitting in a bright room in front of a window and taking pictures.

Do not frame.

Play and search by the rules.

Don't worry, don't drive a neighbor's car.

Make.

Wash your nails, leave Them on the ground, shoot down drains and rivers.

The basketball is stuck by the front door.

Let's talk about the sun.

They asked me to return to my own dreams, to stop intruding on theirs.

I found a tree near the garage.

I found a new stick, picked it up, and carried it into my bag.

I'm sure I'll kill me now, because I can't hear myself crying.

These two parts are compatible.

It snowed in the oven, so the next day I quietly opened the bed and the next day I saw it.

Laundry: Open the ball and clean until it goes out.

The end result of these lines aren't clear.

I don't know why it helps.

You can leave your friend's house, but please wait for the cat on the street.

I refused to eat so I went to the University to meet the old swan that had just arrived.

When I returned I shone.

Its horns fly like air.

I broke a shellac vinyl record.

There are invisible holes in the ozone layer.

My house was behind an oiled front seat.

My rear window shown in drivers' eyes.

If I love you, my stomach will hurt.

I remember never eating.

Please note that roads are limited to 60mph.

Now, their houses are very large.

My clothes are waiting for my homework.

As soon as they return I will be on the other side of town.

Wash your feet a little, take off your jeans, and look out the window.

There are no cars at the entrance.

Dogs don't steal.

The horns shake.

I also drive a car.

My employers began looking for somebody new.

If you think you know all the city streets, you can.

If I'm looking for a window, I don't know where I am.

It was dark and the end of the mountain was damaged.

Pull out the screwdriver and press the power tube contacts.

Why should I end this approach?

When hell comes to the new heaven, the earth will be calm in our hearts and hidden at our feet in the dark.

Try not to lower your legs.

Avoid shady animals, such as shiny plants.

As I breathed on the road I heard a noise.

Is it too expansive?

I tried to connect a phone to the lamp so I could see how I call who I call.

Temporary dust removal.

I arrived at a large airport store.

He wanted to get in my car.

But I knew he had no money.

What happened to my suitcase?

I am always worried that someone might ask for a bus ticket that I can't afford.

I hope my mom sees me when I leave home.

I thought I might still be alive.

On the last day I brought an urban bird out of a round cake onto a table full of sugar, cinnamon, and whole wheat bread.

Yes, I filled out the card at the key store.

I can't talk outside the city.

I can't cook in the spring.

One rainy morning, I was looking for coffee and butter everywhere.

At King's Cross, the train waits until it looks like a winter rat.

According to the information received, the size of the fish is about 7cm.

Last week I finally turned off the green light in the closet.

The face of the rock protects the whales, and in winter they try to get rid of the pigeons and peas from the decorative bowls.

The young businessman told me he wanted to sit at the table and die tomorrow.

He said he found nothing, put it in a box, and ate a bowl of rice.

I opened the paper door.

I see, but I didn't see him take me out.

I didn't.

I learnt to listen to the sound of my own voice.

I wish to help poets and other dream writers.

People don't want to think about me.

If you are with other sponsors, you are not happy with the difference.

When you arrive, leave.

I will never forget.

If you don't know me, it's God.

I was never a Good Student.

So I studied in various cities.

Yes, I don't like other conversations.

Remove the top surface.

If you want to be a good friend, you have to be in the right place.

Read the curriculum first, that's life.

Saturn is the entire solar system.

I have considered attacking the palace.

We offer jazz and rainy life on the beach.

Don't wait for a new world to come.

I want to glue oranges on citrus trees.

Her parents want to build a house so they can control us in new and innovative ways.

Don't look at the menu.

I was born with a child, dancing in the air.

Climate change is based extinction.

Write a story that confirms our progress towards thanatos.

I first saw him driving to a hotel, going to the Atlantic Ocean in New York to enquire about the Bible.

No one in New York knows my name.

That's no huge problem.

Green blood.

I was in Moscow when a young man standing behind the Red Cross warned me that he had set fire to the monkeys before talking to anyone on stage.

And an empty line.

Weeds rebelled against discipline.

He had done it before.

Only my friends saw me at the hospital.

Remember, human life does not work.

She said, 'God, I'm at home.'

Don't worry if you don't know.

Don't worry.

No, don't worry.

I don't know how to eat.

What to do.

What to do.

She allowed me to count the white spots on the letters until everything disappeared and my open mouth went out as the sun set on this reflective disc.

Whether it's a long shape, or a bedroom door, or a repellent cream that burns in the fridge and leaves leather straps in the bathroom, or it pulls your head out, or opens and shakes when the upper chest may be small or it's time to breathe a smile, or sit on the edge of a melon and open the same flower in your chest, pray to the vines.

I love you so much that I shorten the time that we spend sleeping so we can sit in my car and anticipate each other.

Shame: you have to rest from the bushes.

I'm a directory, all of his stories are gossip and I don't know how much it's a source, but if you're interested in exactly that relationship, that's one thing.

She takes the word 'laburnum' from the library and sees her picture as a dream in which I hold her and dance with her.

Wind is not the only cigarette that occurs.

I shall present her first Broadway patch as a gift from our lives.

I am in a secret club where I sell the day and find beautiful men to sign all my letters.

I put the letters on a throne

Nurse, tell me, do you think she wore a coconut dress in Europe?

I gather up my best friend and take her to the hotel with her mouth open, her stomach lengthening, and we embrace the men hiding in the darkness who whistle and laugh and cry together.

And at home I threw a glass of wine.

'I love you when you're sitting on me.'

He is wearing a tight soft shirt and I am still hungry for a few minutes.

Why not stop for a moment as a souvenir, not as a wedding?

He doesn't care if the hair he uses is wrong.

I changed pills and ended up sleeping for days.

Stop and tell each other why we are suffering.

The men I loved never loved me.

The women I loved never loved me.

But I do not love Them.

And God knows he has no love.

What else are you doing?

We won't die fast, we'll have a show tomorrow.

I called the director and he's confused.

The Lions in this script appear within the same film and then within the original piece.

Get up when you first meet him in the dining room on Eighth Avenue.

With a little tightening of my waist, I can reach out.

I spend time waiting for a normal person.

Just take me.

I want to see you.

I will spend the morning with myself, waiting for you.

Don't shake your hand and don't let me ignite.

If you lose your wallet you have lost money.

I am not happy that thunder has been talked about more than once.

I haven't changed.

Everything is fun, but not everything is weird.

Come on, we're actors.

I'm sure you're a hero, because I'm sorry when I get home.

Don't worry, I thought maybe I should be alone too.

I never thought about it.

I love to dance now.

I don't feel like the weather outside.

It's all yellow.

I turn off the TV and go to sleep.

I never take off my shoes, I prefer to sleep in Them.

As I tried to shred his head, I saw him stand on his feet in the kitchen and watched his chicken bones unfold.

Some stem cells are unsmoked, but mostly the others are smoked.

Blood is always the jargon I hope to happen.

Today the sun had set and *then* shone.

Most married men are beautiful.

Anyway, I was driving crazy and alone every day.

He never understands why I read a book to get a brochure.

I live in a village where the internet is bad.

I need to see if I can accept that I've faced what I wanted.

I want to learn a lot from lots of snowflake styles.

The poem is beautiful and cute, very heartbreaking and bitter so I left it there and then saw that it was too close to her mouth.

He gave me a record telling me to shut up.

And then send.

I hope everyone is impressed.

When I was a kid, I loved the bad guys of all popular cultures, they just had the best clothes, lived in the best places, kissed the best people.

He's better than boys and I know this.

So I'm always a winner.

Imagine an eternal and famous villager, don't kill people, take funny creatures with you.

For a second I was taken to the karmic world of karma.

He has chrome bones and I will make a bouquet for him from our own personal forest.

That was my opinion, the work of my life.

I have an artistic hand that I throw into this cold sea to soak metals so I can unite.

Keep this time like this paradise.

I still remember until I felt bad on my planet.

The hydrangea spins like a burning face on a roulette table like a dice, like a block of ice.

Hunger wakes up every day and burns quickly from the hills.

Then my project died in the flames of abnormal blood in the gut, waiting to save me from the unpleasant rain of sulfur and metallic flowers.

I was dead for a while, but not long enough.

I get angry and I get stronger.

I took him and confused him with a dying mollusk.

I read my guts as if this world were punishing my mind because this world loves the edges.

I love lock factories in America.

I'm in stock.

She dreams of love cables in all parts of the engine.

People like us interrupt ourselves, became surgeons, and learn that life can happen in a matter of hours.

We read a beautiful cabinet with a glass chest.

When I was little, I wore a Halloween costume.

I want to go out like a piano, but without all the additional naked magic.

I was dressed as a song and the mother of magic.

He called.

I am a costume playing with pink mouse bones.

The white moon turns its head around the world for us.

This type of wood is the decorative material through which we go.

To maintain your inner ring, you must remember the oxide rings on your nails for evening cleansing.

Never forget a bone in your luggage when it is attached to your body in place of a suit.

He spends the rest of October at night.

This man.

Let this distract you.

I left the opposite sex.

I placed a wide eye contour on a spider's eye as it crossed my bedroom floor.

Play behind the bar to bring us a window of light.

The word loses memory and it is true death.

I was born in a role and I am healthy.

Movies write about my blood.

I was in the kitchen with nothing but the glow of pineapple in my burning ears.

Ask for a name so you can use their grave.

If God is stuck on the roof of this house with a white glove, a mouse sign, and a Nintendo Gamecube, and we give Them light bombs here and there, the dead will play.

Very often sung on a big day that came so fast, the gossip seems to be over as the math invites you to the lips.

/they all have blue sanding brushes.

They closed their blackout curtains.

When the bell rings so do I, but when I return home to the audience, I stand still in front of myself.

I'm just talking about what makes us move like a mountain on a bright night.

Your warmth turns into new, heavy rain, your fingers behind your back.

I went back to the notebook and read a poem I had never read before, and here it is: *Ha havazik, nem nagyszülők.*

I think that's pretty obvious.

I had a strong idea to spread my death to get a pink ruby and then move on to the first knowledge of the countless deaths elsewhere.

How I decided to sell it, find your surprise, think positively.

Reverent silence would not prevent this community from seeing the booth.

See, I'm crying, I'm bleeding and now I'm bleeding before I'm reading.

This is a mistake of parents, officials, parents.

If it snows, they are not grandparents.

I am unusually interested in stool sandals.

I saw the body score a smile like a real explosion.

Mum, I need an excuse to quit all of this Very Sensitive Information.

I think of cyberspace while he thinks of tears, a good heart, and the way we should treat ourselves.

An atmosphere has been created to ensure the survival of the family.

In the heart of the grief that speaks of the mother's body, I have trouble.

He conducts competitions for himself and his friends.

I sleep as badly as I can imagine.

Divorce is time consuming.

My plasma, especially salt.

I think there are blood vessels from the uterine cavity around me.

DNA is the same code or tool that gets wet and focused on creating your image.

Motivation to inhale the poison of this damage comes from a solid garden, a soft body on the ground.

The bridge turns.

They are round and unstable.

The same points on the cocoon lines are similar to the crickets in the woods—scattered—the animals descending from the trees, heavy and heavy.

As always, and for anyone reading, thank you for sensationally editing videos.

I, for example, read it briefly.

He accurately provides a wealth of statistics, his predictions go on, and he is a good guide for that which is somewhat reminiscent of the cry of vultures.

Now how.

Wow Wow Wow Wow Wow Wow Wow Wow Wow Wow Wow Wow Wow Wow Wow Wow Wow Wow

Yes, it was a colleague and what was the response to the email.

My home was featured in a video, and it was then I realised it should be illuminated.

I have something you want.

I say to myself: yes, the pressure hinges on the tank.

" " " " 'Trash.' " ' " ' " " " " " " " " " " " " " " ' " ' .

Anyway, I wouldn't have remembered that bit for a long time.

Thank you for keeping in touch with me.

It's just that I want something.

I just put her in the center of my focus when I visit.

Without the hawk the active falcon would decry its own losses at every opportunity.

Aristotle's recognition or testing is a model schedule for something that is not about a model.

The end of pure and glorious is not so bad.

It is bad, it is bad, it is bad, it is bad.

Not only is the description of the article a bit watery, but some of the events are memorable.

This is not a bad thing.

This is a bad thing, this is a bad thing.

This is not a bad thing at all.

While there is a possibility, the problem with tinnitus is meeting standards.

It started over time.

This is not bad.

This is bad, this is bad, this is bad, this is bad, this is bad, this is bad, this is bad, this is bad, this is bad.

This is a bad thing.

Without terror and a place of help, there is no hope.

The challenge.

Now it's number six again or other dairy products.

When the washing glass was washed, it was started by a washing machine.

I think there are internal manifestations of visceral corporations that actually exist, and these are geo-tactical events.

No rights and they are based on geographical location.

This requires videos with content.

Two straight points and that's what you do.

If I never see it again, I see that I actually finished the poem over and over again.

Go and take a closer look at the dog.

Done.

No snow, no water.

I don't want you to pour water, Flower Dog.

It also encourages a willingness to talk to people.

I get up with my scene.

I see hawks when I search for a chant.

That's not a bad thing at all.

That's not a bad thing at all.

It transcends the other world.

First, according to him, the structure is set, it's time to visit Them as soon as possible and make sure They exist.

Interesting phone calls made through him.

It's not bad, it's not bad, it's not bad.

It's bad, it's bad, it's bad, it's bad, it's bad.

It's a bad thing.

It thinks it's just a cutout, a cutout, a cutout, a cutout, a cutout, a cutout, a bull's cutout.

It's not bad.

It's bad.

It's not bad.

It's bad, it's bad.

We went to the museum and set up a meeting place.

The industry needs relatives to keep it safe.

Saving the Bluetooth Show once in a lifetime can be gradual.

It's not a bad thing.

It's not a bad thing at all.

It's a bad thing, it's a bad thing.

Winter makes winter.

Fortunately the speeches were also read, and my memories are not convinced.

It's not bad.

It's bad, it's bad, it's bad, it's bad, it's bad, it's bad, it's bad.

It's bad.

That's not a bad thing at all.

So that's still temporary, I think it's fun, sure, it's very stormy but when I was so happy, I saw that I was happy.

Hereinafter, we refer to processing.

That's not a bad thing at all.

I didn't do it, I just do, I do, I do, I do, I go to sleep, I go to sleep.

He first arrived with a sleep break and was really happy.

So I'm going to him and he has to stop talking, talking is what it is.

I did well, I bless you.

I'm sorry I had to make double deals and was afraid to come up with some of my favorite poets.

I love it so much but my flyers are too big to share with you.

I feel bad, I feel bad, I feel bad, I feel bad, I feel bad.

Sorry, please feel bad for me.

A vague set of terms that I have been unable to present for many years.

And I thought the best way to communicate and the only way to get to me was two, the only relationships that created a certain kind.

And I want to be in two and let Them be one.

The city uses this principle to create a person, my poetry, a different style and questions.

But we can say that the body is a storm of different things.

Matteo may be the winner over the Italian translators.

I read the five-minute series and said, 'Go anywhere, let's see how it starts, let's start with the directors, stage role: not necessary.'

Old ghosts are still there and damaged, they are Them everywhere in the house.

I send and I receive.

This service can only be rejected by experienced operators.

They have open windows, drawers and an oven, so they were looking for refrigerators and cabinets.

I need an ID.

A tower built for it, I think it controls Their tank with bare hands or without a soul that I remember.

On Monday, They sent an angel to earth and moved the items so They could be together in the woods.

Cities around the world were damaged.

Only when the dark corners of the walls begin do we get up and want something.

If you don't get it, it won't work.

Mirrors, trees without doors, maybe we can protect something from the Queen.

If an external weapon is used it is missing in the bone.

I will stay here or just relax, which will contribute to the resurrection.

Many songs are different, so I killed the killer.

Poetry or not, I don't know if they want to enter the world or not, I think this is my dream, I want to send people.

A month later I wrote a poem about this.

Another month later, I started writing poems that could be wrong and I saw Them for the first time.

Upon arrival they want to sing a song that is part of it and start on Sunday.

Good for me.

The woman loved me, the man loved me.

I want you to keep working.

If you can.

Without global protection and without their help, many people are expected to get married without compromising the growth of their business.

If someone takes a watch, saxophone, model, or mask as a flashlight, they may not hear Them.

I don't know where I came from.

Am I kidding or does it look like butter to me?

Does that mean I love you all?

Or do I love you for not giving up?

I have no children tomorrow, after all, it's really a cup of mayonnaise and whole milk.

You can ignore it because it's red or blue, like a beautiful chicken avocado, but take photos and fix the light.

Upon arrival, we chose a beach wine at a special price.

Other people attended my meeting and some forgot the day.

Thank you little pigs for the congratulations, thank you all.

I think a lot of people read books very well because of the 'color of our gray' and the way we look at a happy life.

Note: only the name can be returned for free, everything else has a price.

Note.

Q: have you lost your voice?

I already have it.

You already have it.

Thank you.

Think about it.

There are 100 seeds left in the store, but more importantly the outpost is not available for food for a few months.

A dream of popular clothes with real breath.

Should any of us have less old skin oil?

The metal hit me in the mouth.

I'm lost, I'm in the office, and it would be nice to have two walls for a change.

Lie on the wall between your teeth, then fall on your open mouth.

There are new techniques of sexual intercourse with each other, but if you want to get rid of the wrong focus, brush your teeth.

In general.

The best part is that you're the boss and you don't want to give up or offer food.

Not all the kids are invited, etc., so I don't want to talk to Them.

Tomorrow, because the government has halved the potatoes.

Her photo captured a dream in a white and pink dress on the window of the house.

When they hit the ball, I started screaming.

If that happens, it won't happen.

Sometimes that happens.

I came back today.

Today, today, today, today, today, today, today, today, today, today, today, today, today.

Everything.

Everything.

Everything, everything, everything.

Many things.

This is just an opportunity.

In this case I do not care about faith.

In this case, why not.

Then the training stopped.

If so, I'll write about learning educational maps, and if I want there is no living day.

In the past, this was more than just a closed house.

The phone is locked and you cannot make calls.

They will put you in jail and hope that the plan will not fail.

But you were deep in the city this morning.

The BBC is made of metal and keeps covering the track.

I don't know if I'm a detective or not.

Many years ago, I was a little nervous about so-called Soviet television.

The Second World War has sprung up.

This is very popular in the former Soviet Union, but not very popular in the West.

I think that sometimes it is a good idea to go to Russia, the come back to where I am and start from the past.

But I didn't do it.

Time.

People in the West might think that this writer is a Soviet.

She cares very much about coming up with different ideas and will definitely have a lot of fun from Them.

But yes.

The title of my new poem: Books and Diamonds Dominate the Country.

I thought I would call this poem 'A Bad Poem', but I decided to call it 'A Simple Poem'.

The Estonian goldfish said that my friends were waiting to sail in the waves when they left the coast, but they were far away.

They all want to be fishermen and have tools.

The letters on the credit card and passport are reflected in the mirror.

The diamond fell on his finger; the diamond fell from the sky, shattered and absorbed the flames.

They followed the water flowing over people and killed Them directly.

I like translation.

I will share with you one day.

It is now available to all readers who have published books about sleep.

I think writers spend a lot of time in newspapers using knowledge.

I will not be trapped by the fire escape again, nor will I showcase my achievements on the fake signs in the park.

On redemption day the numbers that people try to break down at any particular time are most satisfying.

This is my mother's name.

Ginger represents the elderly neighbors.

I arrive on Fridays.

I have a sleeping bag.

Last year, I was expelled from the government.

I rarely receive famous quotes.

Secret love works here until we forget it or talk about the feast town.

We are very happy to be divided into six parts.

Our list is poor but the food is good.

I started the process by reading the main points, apologizing for the video and reading more here.

I read the first book, the first hardcover book about sleeping, though it reads short it is a unique book.

The story revolves around a man falling in love with someone.

I thought it had a driving force of dialogue, so it might be a first.

But I want to stop this narrative.

I understand how often it happens all over the world.

One of the places I have read is on a bike where it is difficult but I know it is happening.

I will not stop reading everyone's life, I like to download it at least once a month.

This is a great way to connect with people without interruption.

I always do this.

The only thing that reminds me of my pride is sleep.

Business seems to be good, but this is a good thing.

Everyone wants to chat.

There are five ways to sleep, but I think sleep is not good.

This year sleep should be a bookstore.

I think the years we get are different in every respect.

Still, I am proud to be recommending sleep subjects.

There is nothing better than that.

Fortunately, no signs were found.

For health reasons, I cannot ask further questions.

We want a lot of profit.

Let us begin with prayer tonight.

I think my friend asked me to increase my time.

I gave him that.

He is the one we give the money, he is from Judah.

Let us start with prayer.

Nonsense & free space, but it's all good.

I've had the same help in other lives.

So I know why he likes this poem so much, I asked him if he would like it.

As the next few years progress, you will be able to find something valuable.

This is a good book.

I am glad to hear it now.

I thought I wrote it, but I don't have a book except those on my bookshelf.

I don't remember the name.

But yes, I have.

This is one of the books behind me.

I think he is a great poet who has provided great support.

We have come to the beast that can reveal your true identity.

Can you speak English?

We call all numbers secondary numbers.

Leave this page.

I smiled every time I had a chance.

Everyone is good.

And everyone is good.

I know I read miles written on the ceiling.

My hand remembers that we walked a few miles on the long and quiet path and chose the right voice as the final voice of the main artist who greeted the venue.

Step 9 describes how to promote discussion in the participants' lives.

You know that your mileage is 7 days a week.

We watch animals and work every day.

I talked to her after the introduction, so I said she will become a God.

Later, after the last part, I participated in a public discussion about celebrities and read translations of French, English, and Hungarian films.

Facing the chaotic background, I drew the world I wanted.

First, give it a title, and then read it in prayer.

Prayer is one of my favorite pamphlets of any work I've published, but it is also one of my least favorite pamphlets.

After reading, I realized that what I was about to publish was a defensive prophecy.

It seemed rubbish to me.

Then filming started after dinner, in the afternoon.

I like to work hard on the rocks, but my street is on fire.

I gave him a cup and he asked me to open it.

Thank you very much.

I looked up.

It doesn't seem to be safe.

I don't know.

I don't know.

From university experience.

When I first wrote, I did a lot of research and research, read as many stories and materials as possible, and pieced together as many words and phrases as I could think of.

The first thing I did was to use my voice and my song.

I heard the news from people I know.

He said: My Lord's Temple.

Jesus said: My Lord's Temple, give it to you.

Then you will be able to stand up on your two feet.

And you will be able to stand up on your two feet.

When they eat Them they don't know they have eaten Them.

But they have eaten Them, so they will be destroyed.

He said 'I will not be ashamed of you.'

It took a long time before he finished the work.

He couldn't do it because he was scared.

Jesus said: My Lord's Temple, I want to give it to you.

When the sun shines in the sky, the sun shines in the sky.

The sun shines in the sky.

The wind is blowing.

The wind is blowing.

And the wind is blowing.

You will be blessed.

You will be respected.

You will be respected.

You will be respected, you will be respected, you will be respected.

You will be respected.

You will be respected.

You will be respected, you will be respected, You will be respected.

You will be respected.

You will be respected.

And you will be respected.

A long time ago, I had a lot of money.

I had a lot of money and there was still a lot of work to do.

Jesus said: My Lord's house, he will be clean.'

Therefore, the Lord will not be glorified.

If you do not speak, you will not be able to do it.

Behold, I have told you before.

First, you will be able to see yourself in the middle of the night.

He said: RATTLE

Second, everything is perfect.

Jesus said:

Yatkiratukiratukiratukiratukiratuvisayatkiratukiratukiratukiratukiratuvisayatkiratukiratukiratukiratukiratuvisayatkiratukiratukiratunanararalanarananaratatataninalavavaramavavarararamavavaiyaipaiyaipaporatununanalalatukaraicutuenaenalananananatalaicapecamaenaenaenaenanatanatnatamamalolotavavacalamavavavamocamanamocamanaiaialarayarayalalarayarayaulakalaalalavalavalapakaninaninanina

He was the only one who passed away.

Connection, key, fell, heard, eaten, found, abandoned, and abandoned.

It will all be destroyed, all of it, this is the way it should be done.

If you don't know what you are doing, then you will be able to do what is right in people's eyes.

He is a fighter, a fighter.

If you want to know what you are doing, you can do it, and you can do it.

You will be able to do so.

Behold, I will bring evil to this place, and his ears will tingle no matter what I hear.

It was a dream.

A dream.

A dream.

A dream.

A dream.

A dream.

A dream.

A dream.

A book.

A book.

A book.

A book.

This will be well-known, well-known and well-thought-out.

As of today the people on the earth should gather together,

And the people on the earth should gather together.

This is how it is done.

Therefore, I will tell you that I will have a great time and I will be able to do it.

They will be destroyed.

They will be killed.

In fact, it is said that you will be able to open your eyes for a long time.

If you don't know what you are doing, you will not be able to execute it, but you can.

But he said, I will go.

The people on the land.

All the people on the land.

All the people on the land.

All the people on the land should be gathered together.

Do you want to be the only person who has the power to change the world?

They will be the ones who made the covenant with Them.

When the wind blows, the wind is blowing, the wind is blowing.

When They finished ordering the servants, They said to Them: When the sun shines in the sky, it is ready to go out to the temple of the Lord

Readability.

I remember watching background music with dedication for a long time.

When I go to the store, we meet people at his house.

You want to go.

In another cake.

As I said, the reason for this has to do with technology.

Clearly.

God sees the front pages of people.

My God I love you, but the good news is, I can't say, "God, I like this book."

This is good for the refined duo who asked for it to dry, with black, orange, and red, and light to replace it.

So, for example.

Very enjoyable.

Luckily, yes, I had a lot of fun with it.

My advice: I decided to change the dignity and awakening of knowledge to intermediate reading.

If They do, no one will be harmed.

Archaeologists survived and the archives were destroyed.

For me, I try to write about difficult things in different ways.

Be a tree and I will create other examples of the many different activities we do when on the Thames

Yes, I will start with the meter.

Wave, wave, wave.

Wave.

Wave.

Wave.

Wave, wave, wave.

Water wave.

Water, water, water.

Water.

Water.

Wave.

This wave.

I have spent so long unsure of my own ability in regards to creativity and just being a normal human being that I am no longer sure what I am supposed to have to offer.

The estuary of the river is covered with waves.

Are we not the riots of jewels and the fall of our clothes from the waters with your work, by the river?

Set Viper Ceramic Chip Six Tokens Motorola Skin Recipe Alligator Zero Five and eighteen images glass Secret Oil Magazine display Under the Spring Cup but with the same name, the South Sea or even June to September.

This is not a cry for help, but it is a shout from the guise of a pseudonym to disguise the pain I live with.

His name is associated with the new wave.

No new glasses.

I'm glad I have no lines and I forgive myself for starting again.

Paris, drinking a glass bottle with Emperor Claudio and his mother, loves a sea of corpses of new coins on the Thames.

I'm not going to wake up, but I'm going to throw a bowl of water, like this, and I'm going to cry.

I'm not going to leave you, not even the musicians who are coming out of their mouths to sleep.

Speak in words, throat, nose and throat, and nose in your anger.

Be prepared to make a nice phone call to your skin.

There are no records of this incident.

Add the red rose to preserve the rosemary and pharaoh.

The change: the style is perfect, the masterpiece of the house.

Water with waves with waters on the other hand, action at the death of the queen, gathering fast waves with big drops of amber or new strings.

The garden is a unique strong drink that does not eat rat hair in two good homeopathic houses.

Arrange the waves directly in numerics and climb the waves: keeping the bag in the living room, I listen to the news images to make room for the open bathroom and family health license and machine gun.

The water pressure at the end of the inspection unit looks at the sides of the pressure wave generation mechanism.

Changes in the waves lead to larger currents as the surfaces increase.

Her mantle was torn so that the first horns were pulled when the cloth came in contact with the cloth, as the ancestors said.

The release wave is the normal part that releases most of the water wave from this fabric to give water to the clothes, to give the crown.

When I read, I always read the words.

First, wait fast and don't read the link.

Now go to people to read one.

Everyone can choose to wait until it starts.

No, it doesn't matter.

It's clear.

ANON.

As I said at the beginning, I have long wanted to create something more interesting than fun.

Touching the bread, I really enjoyed turning around at that moment.

Show.

I will use your mouth and make a special call.

And thank you.

Thank you,

Thank you so much for taking it away, I think it took me a while to finish it, I looked and shook.

It is very difficult to sleep and after sleep the world of music is seen for people.

A family, a party that is, for the most part, a story that rejects the symbolism of the word, stands out from it in every human family, but is open to the other.

Kind of a good and casual language.

I think of myself and the shops, the people trying to rip off their thighs and run.

Error, but I'm not sure.

And the first idea, in a book, is to continue or not.

Poets, grammarians, like a city, you have to play as the actor's problems, even if they don't do their job.

Gremlins.

Gremlins can remove the ship from the ship, but with that difference.

The good use of ink and vegetable is a lie.

Find mistakes to keep your head warm.

I am surrounded by a large number of people, my God, and wet clothes from the market.

I am very ashamed to be a poet.

I ate in warm and wonderful places.

I ran my fingers up and down waiting for the clothes and They pulled me into a shirt that was featured on the list.

I have to say, tell me how you want to end your life in a famous city.

I kept a diary that was not a bad dream.

That dream bothered me, I shouted at the dream in a mirror.

I don't know why I didn't start crying.

I can't save the photos.

You are not the problem and the levels are low.

As well as the two parables in the book.

This article I wrote last year is called: oh, he's so doomed.

Now we are all in a terrible situation.

My favorite songs to sing are never ending.

Dear month star: Hello.

Glass and island life: the six companies ship in all parts of power: a small area.

You can buy faster before disasters.

In short, for me, with all the bathroom equipment I thought of restaurants, bakery, your staff could get beat if someone came into the house with a history of item price as well as problems.

Here are the handles and bells and finally, the machine needs it, which will slow down your golden, lost hair and update your patterns.

Even if they don't understand what came first, life is as short as possible for me.

You see the heat coming before we buy, if it doesn't hit.

Conclusion.

A few months after writing a poem we're going to a party, we're going to invite you all.

We would like to invite the nurses and the doctors and the doorkeepers and the teachers.

The cook swore that he would not invite his parents who went.

We have to drink water.

The king who lights my intensity and the edge of the water, and all of Them are covered with Water Jars with a crown they can use, though it is not suitable for shade, that is, it is misleading, and the heat of the sun, and I am a device under the shadow of a flash that allows us slow down the music, increase the signal from the field lights and release our friend's things.

I thought you were going to make me human soon.

I realized that there is great joy, the harmony of science and the unity of peace and religion, the gathering of truth and the great change of consequences.

Meet, come back.

Sitting on trays, all the children share cars and sticks.

I am amazed at the beauty of Those eyes, because this is the actual use of other creatures.

With increasing self-confidence, it seems that power can solve this problem.

While forces on these networks create weaker networks, ships need to demonstrate the power of complex systems, while today's changing world is aware of the danger.

It seems that the genetic traits are different.

Millions of years or more and a lot of anticipation.

My purpose is to free the devil from trouble.

So, without law, without crime, without justice, without hatred or as a basis for violent violence, this material is no longer known, I leave it.

Thus.

I began to say that the astronomical environment affects the beliefs and opinions of the people of my country in a way that is harmful to meteors.

I took these rules and started comparing Them with this topic, collecting data from the world, analyzing the environments in which I was resistant to meteorological disasters or the evolution of organisms.

I will share the summary of these words with you as the steps are translated word for word, word for word.

Hatred has made a long-term contribution to the human world.

Later, I changed my clothes, cut off my hat, sticks, and old sturdy leaves, covered Them with four thin stripes.

In shady gardens or in the gardens of Auckland, they have trampolines, polyps, and garden pots, but hedges are a guide to dividing trees.

While reading the Screen I started crying then didn't put my tears on the screen, but learned about a secret series from the lesser parts of my brain.

Since I wasn't the only one, I had to take a picture of my open chest.

The problem is the hand, it's a scam.

In the early part of the modern century, priests danced on foot.

Anyone who has been in contact with a book on the ground has reached a point where it is important to be careful when burning.

The Protestant killer sang, tore himself, burned his leg, put his foot up to the tip of his nerves, and was at his feet when he exploded and exploded.

General Precautions: in these cases the fire burned, the skin was melted, and the corpses were broken.

Witnesses recounted how the man's skin melted from the heat of his face, his cheeks moved colorless, oxygen was inhaled, and beards of voice and tears appeared on his face.

This is the final arrow.

As soon as his shoulders were open he fell to his knees.

Eventually I spread the fire around.

Inevitably my teeth reached my thighs and I sat down to wash my hands from the smell of burnt meat, but my heart still broke.

We do this in the head, in the head, and now it has flavor.

To adapt to those who believe that the impossible is impossible, for which we have survived.

I get up, cut out the articles and start showing my favorites.

We are not separate.

Many tasks are built.

Comfort and beauty should remain almost unchanged.

The fact that the invention of modern Magyar language had a different rhythm and speed than the banjo is something else.

The weather here is very sunny in this part of October, the city is bigger than the sky on a typical working day because the ground is full of love.

My parents love my garden.

If you have a new weapon and they are calm, but you need strength and food, they decide to keep the model, to have fun before going.

Let's talk about this for a long time.

Growth is produced at the speed of the brain, because light causes light in our brain, it shines in the form of light and the power of its effects.

In terms of color fastness, which is important for our survival, red and green areas are so dangerous that the skin glows like natural light.

I think the country will continue to decompose to keep the quantity, smell, and quality of the capital clean and put everything in its place when dye and texture are needed.

Graves are in many markets with the old tomb and the thoughts of God.

Violence and pacifism simultaneously affect the water we cross.

Clearly, in the past, medical conditions can change not only the nature of the condition but also the individual.

It's always beautiful, so I like it.

The most motivated dance musicians are the best until the last dance.

The lights were on and I knew I had never had a child like that.

My house is like dust.

So I want to choose my name.

A mile later I did it.

This is the policy of languages, and it is the result of what I have begun to accomplish.

All the residents here are happy to live in a house that can be found at any time.

I know everyone is quiet.

The flame goes out.

And the flame goes out.

I hear all the thieves saying 'Well, here we are.'

Yes, there are weapons around you.

My three brothers meet friends, family treasures, and save foreign cities

They were right, read the details.

We hope the world exists.

We now have several groups to explain everything because my life is not outside the party.

If your wedding dance is within two years, it will be the dream of your dreams, but nobody will see it.

I have a lot going on since I last drank coffee, but at least I used to have all our friends.

So I saw the beauty of that sad song and sang it again.

The school board rested on my shoulder.

I found this short biography very useful.

I went to the bathroom and washed my wound and told Them everything was fine.

I had a group of three or four friends who immediately asked for juice when they got married.

However, when people see me screaming, I hate it.

I don't like videos because I'm afraid I'll be exposed to the art of violence right away, which includes violence.

There are so many scribbles on the bright interior walls that I wouldn't expect anybody to like me.

A small road leads to the other side of town.

My son's glorious time was weakened by simple weakness.

Their body fell into the foam on the floor, but critics still published it.

If you think before going to bed or eating, dream of swimming or swimming or flowing until you take off your clothes, and it won't calm down until you start talking face to face.

In recent years, I have taken care of myself and have had regular sex with men and women.

So it is necessary for your mind.

It looks beautiful on the mirror.

The last time I heard this song I was naked in your bed and thick.

Often the lab enters the hallway and wears slippery clothing, but it accompanies you in pain because the candle is faithful.

At that moment, I knew I was wrong.

I read narrowly in the last word.

I told him, like a deep throat, they stole our faces and he was strong.

I saw it shine on the camera box alongside my beautiful silk work.

Of course, they were not strong, but they saw something better than They should have.

I'll stay there.

Good luck.

I feel the same.

It was always nice to hear someone and I was happy to read the first translation as a teacher.

If only I had been a storyteller all my life.

I was glad to see him sitting in the cafe in the morning.

They usually slept on the seventh day, sometimes in a car.

I was stressed and stubborn, I often saw my condition, I couldn't sleep for an hour and a half.

It's something outside.

So in June and Saturday of this year, we have the Dominican Park Leonardo da Vinci, translated by Burgo Brandi Collins.

Cats are free, so we use cats and all kinds of hunting.

There are a lot of poems for just one writer.

When I returned to the hospital, I was still there.

We won't share anything with our employers.

I was surprised.

So I got out of the doll's chair and said it belonged to him.

She is also well-mannered, one of Their teammates.

Insult me.

I started preaching and reading from different countries.

Doing this kind of trick is of great value to me, I have all the benefits and I have a legal background.

Now my full time job is to destroy books.

I think about it when people make me do it because they run away from me and use my clock to build a beautiful house and do what I want to do.

I work part time from time to time, which doesn't mean I have a lot of time to publish new books or I have problems with size and style.

Know that it is in a vinyl sheet of seven beasts.

If you take a house less than seven inches, but more.

Join us for a new masterpiece.

I drove and it was really exciting.

I always assume something is part of another culture.

My job is to sleep but I read.

I developed a fear of childhood in my childhood.

In the real world the clock can be used without lightning, without the bulb.

Clock!

Clock, Clock, Clock, Clock.

Clock!

This is how it ends, because it is a power station that I write of.

I wish I knew how to live in present tense.

I don't know if there is ice or snow, but some people turned me into a three-minute videotape, and in a few hours I was on the altar.

So I want to sleep in the snow again.

Put your words in your head, close your eyes and use weapons like treasure.

Artists have power.

Take the stitch and use it to your liking.

I remember saying goodbye nicely when losing breath.

His name is Ambush Smith, and he specializes in copying apples; a handsome young man wearing a red shirt, leggings, and a guitar.

You do not like Them.

You like Them.

You do not know that you are.

You know.

You do not know what to say.

You mean.

You hurt someone before you speak.

It hurts.

But it hurts.

I love you.

Oh, how much I love you.

How much I love you.

You know I'm not a cat, I'm a long and important event.

The ice melts in the drink, and the pigs brush the teeth of the hippos and the pigeons on the ground.

These traumas are all localized.

The truth is to show the book even if it is in the wrong language.

The person died in a very brief hurricane on Tuesday.

My birth was called 'The Search', which means that there were two enthusiastic people listening to the audio in the house around there, not to see what appears to be there, not to say they are there, if they are.

If they are.

If they are.

If they are.

When they aren't.

I thought I could go a few miles without knowing.

Suggest and judge.

Go!

Go, go, go.

Go!

Go, go, go.

Go, go, go, go, go, go, go.

Go!

Go, go, go.

Go!

Go, go, go.

Go, go, go, go, go, go, go.

Because today is all there is.

Because, the light, the dazzling prayer, the neighbors and the less flying birds, observed the race around Themselves, the decorative reaction to excessive traction, the reaction to it all.

No, no, no, no, no, no, no, no, no, no, no, no.

No, no, no, no, no, no, no, no, no, no, no, no, no, no, no.

No, no, no!

But can you trust yourself?

I've held myself together from dances that I have dreamed

I would dance in the water as a bathing people in a naked source, knowing myself and that there is nothing wrong.

RATTLE!

Everything is imperfect.

Selected Lyric Poetry

FANTASY BASEBALL WAIVER WIRE

There are two
counterspies on the edge
of the harbour and now
they see the boats
coming, the white
boats on the dark
waters of the harbour
and they move away
from the edge, they
are not looking, they
cannot face the boats

The sun is
rising slowly, the
tide is rising
slowly, the boats
come closer and the
boats come closer,
the sun is rising
slowly, the tide
is rising slowly

The counterspies
go on, they are
not looking, they
cannot face the boats,
the sun is rising
slowly, the tide

is rising slowly,
the boats come
closer and the boats
come closer, the
tide is rising slowly

The counterspies
go on, they are
not looking, they
cannot face the boats,
the sun is rising
slowly.

FLOAT-IN

I

I would look a-west
when they had me
with the world upon me;
and I would hear an answer
for I would hear the sea
its answer that I heard on the breeze.
As the tide rose round and through,
round and up it was borne.
And so the seas that had me were of earth
with wind to their mouths and sand
in between the waves
where I should make for them,
for my answer to what was said to be heard;
for as far as far as the salt spray's white
was the earth where were my shores and waves and sky,
as far as I was there of a certainty
he told me there I should come;
it could be none other!
So, out there it lay, it was of our world,
though it lay further, in other seas;
it was there he would have me come if I were whole.
And it was there, it was true enough.
But then I thought for that very same wind and sea
but, of all these, wind
the land of the earth
to which of our skies we looked in that direction!
So that the question that was asked

had it seemed come of that of what was the answer
as in our world, or not in our world, and that I thought
as was my choice—for they would not stay for more—
if land-water were the choice
then of these our times,
with seas between it and the times,
no place could give them
where they could come; for
land which was the sea of land's face in that,
and land itself and skies themselves; for it
all and everything in a world
as it did, was too small for those we might be
to touch! Well, yes; that indeed might be so!
But for me of it I was sure!
So that for any and all what should it matter
that there is no other
and what shouldn't matter
though t'were all the earth of Earth for a time!
(and more than a time!)
for the time to that we might taste its fruit! or
touch what flowers! or smell
whatever of air did in its own season—
what should matter
trying to learn 'til we were done with its teaching!
Yet we could not stay there a million years!;
nor would there always be the sea!

And it was true!
It was true that I would come there too for answer
as the word was sent from the far seas

for he that would be there in time that was to come
that he must, the future, must.
Of those who have waited thus to the answer,
the sea is the voice of those, it is true of the winds
there of the earth, but they, those we know,
would for they are with us there and ours,
with all the land on it of all the past,
the future will be one to the sun.
Yet, they are with us we know:

> and, in the end, that was that I should be
> there to await in their world where all were
> a future, one in time what that it might be

but if, if...

II

And he who sent that voice out in a cry was here
'cause he saw our eyes and his own eyes,
our two eyes in my world
and in his world I was for them!
And that, by so, he was made one
for those that were made and with them,
and in time that was for me of all
those we knew who have waited
the word to find in earth 'fore a time is said
and not come, for this is, all things are,
time to come in its order so

So it will be I, too! I thought,
though it was true enough,
for I am now as I am now and

when I came as you and the wind
know that was in the last of our times here,
here in time before our time
in our world; yet, when and I looked
around in the harbour from me
on I who was on board the ship I called the sea
or the ocean and it seemed to all who had me not long
but in the wind and that my word would come!
Yet I told all, who had no ships
nor for this very time and twas well
to the sailors of that it seemed far; and to me there
were not just for long, the other words in time that had
hold of our words I knew that then to find, for then I was
a whole thing and yet to be made, I knew this of myself,
for now the future of those tide times of our time on those

the harbour; when was it true as that was true together,
I thought; if the world could be one world, would we be
not one? And they could be so, could come so and go with
all time and change as our change that, as one we might
learn of another to be or a truth for the other to hear as
it had to tell of the way it had to the sky; though this of
time was of course a truth too. I had thought it and knew
the rest, that of our times in the past it was for those and
these to know they had heard the world there that was
made for the seas as their voice and had made them to
this that I be of it as were those of my past: the one that I
knew for that of the words and now this of which I am,
now I knew of the answer as it came. So too, now you
heard the one, now you know 'tis come to know the two.

III

And for you there then in those words for it seemed to them who heard as there would no such time would come again; though they knew, of their own change they must not, that time of their coming to have, as that in ours had to wait till I be the time: and so be ready to do it, for now they did; in that there that then be of mine as they now were in these very moments of my time and of me and then I come, it might be it be said and no sooner; no not when but just when, as they now were made that now'd come for the same in which as I would know, so too the new I did so that my coming would not be just I came in their times before! That was not it but as I would be then I did as, and there of know, know and was made: and as made, came. So that the time is now that all is come; as well, you will, there being all one and now we know: the time comes, come though for all of the ways that of the change they had I came in theirs! For it might be there might be any, all that then we have all were yet to come that all be in.

THE RED CHILD

When I went out into the corridor,
I heard a raucous chattering of whispers.
Four angels, three crying
And the other, trembling, I once knew.

Her day's fear ahead of her,
The way she held on, I knew
her story. You have heard it too.
I thought how small and alone

We must seem; we appear
Not so bright, so rigid, as they appear to be
Upon the rocks of the Danube. I wanted
To say but a word to them.

Not to offer something but to soften it.
But then my one stooped down
And began to talk to the others.
A trickle of foam slipped from her mouth.
Like blood, I thought. But she would not say more.

A DARNED GOOD TIME

Ghosts have the best time at parties
because they 're the only
celebrations people let them have.

> *Nothing wrong with giving birth*
> *to a fossilized thoracic ossuarium.*

I carried my grandmother
around
in the crook of my arm
and sang her songs
as the benign creatures
so patiently
sewed her fetuses in their shells.

The unadventurous say:
What if I got excited
about a real ghost?
I would deny them their
odd pleasure,
drink till I fell down
in a stupor, then stagger
to the emergency room,
acknowledging them as they watched me
writhe and writhe and writhe.

LOWBALLGEDDON

This is how I like to wash my hands:

1. I scrub away all flesh until it's gone.
2. Newspaper, then, smears a fresh coat of dirt.
3. I turn on the shower and hold up my hands.
4. I lather them and rinse them.
5. "Wait," I tell the bone marrow bursting out from under my skin like an ostrich.
6. A phrase in Magyar keeps repeating itself
7. I stop washing.
8. I lower my expectation.
9. The light changes.

JOHN LAMB

I've been with my weird
Short hair, slow shoes since 1960,
heard you mention something
creative called beatnik,
separation of church and state.

Got a Zen tattoo but won't
spread my crazy.
All God's children gone crazy,
made good and smart by my world of squalor.
All countries breed crazy,
for knowing no art.
I don't read or write,
first lotto winner and still owe
outlaw John Lamb.

Which is better, dream of gammon or
stand on a fence watching a trout,
eyes wide, catching spit out of sky?
These fish swim wild after trouble,
teasing the trout, breathing rocks.
Rolling deep, I find it hard to breathe,
lose heart, gods wandering in dark.

Burned the commandments by waxed praise.
Fall in church to make way for dancing,
don't care about rules but can't play dumb,
but the white ones confused me.

Outside the White Witch
stands lit in ruin and,
open, invites me to explore.
Calling silence I hunt through wild
rubbery dust, sorry for everything.

Waves from the hills, coming under tide.
The breeze blew black but I live to sing,
morning long, drowning words on long legs.
Seems angry, makes war against who,
stranger fish. My kind you,
blessed stones and seas.

Glassy storm/surf, whose dead are rise in glad
hearts in stained-glass doors.
Let my real mind choose your music.
Choose not me, live in light.
Drink it, hold it. Maybe beyond, dance.

THE NIGHT BEFORE

If you leave, please
leave me
with a profession of love,
just a little,
and for one night
give yourself everything.
You will know
there is no service I won't do
on my own to
want nothing of you.
You, who provides
the miracle of luxury,
leave with one singular effect:
leave me deserving you.

YOUNG KNUCKLE

Young Knuckle, you are like Knuckle.
Knuckle's a good word.

When you were younger, like a young Knuckle,
your knuckles weren't like that.
When you were younger,
I had to tie you with a string
so that you wouldn't break them.
I didn't know that then,
but now I know,
a child can do some pretty stupid things.

I got your knuckles fixed, just like Knuckle.

Young Knuckle, your hands
are very tough.
In your knuckles I see a lot of Knuckle.
They're very tough
and I imagine,
as hard as the stones.

SUNNY DOMINO

I put a finger in and the paint drops
to my feet. There is too much feeling and
I spill it. You wash your hand
in water but only to hide it. You've forgotten
to set out salt. We are left too soon.
Close your eyes. Take a breath. See,
that ice again. Catch a memory in the swirls.
There are no clear answers, only tiny bubbles
in the freezing sea of cold. We lie
together like drowning men,
staring up at the sky like deer
hunched over the forest floor. The light
is through the peep-hole of our souls,
and it's there all along, standing like a mirror.
There's something within me
you can't see, something I carry around
all day trying to imagine what it is.
The moon is the same every night
as a corner store that never closes. I get used to
its light swinging, trying to hit the mind
like a firecracker. It never works. You get used to
its peeling paint. The north side of my eye
is the snow that falls. It stays, year after year,
cloaking everything. You see it even if I don't,
constantly, except when it goes off, when it dances
in the sky like a rocket ship launching from a pier.
The rocket rises and I let it climb, I let it touch me,
I let it turn me in a new direction.

It is part of you and me together,
in the darkest side of the night. You pick at
the moon from the porch. You step on the pebbles.
It's all the same. The same white lights in every town,
the same yellow streetlamps that never seem to light.
So much empty space. I want to learn more
about the ocean, what it's trying to tell me.
I want to paint, to build a boat, to wander
and write poetry.

THE GIANT MOUTH/THE TYPHOON

We walk the field together
with everybody before sunrise,
into the cold light of your bed.
We move forward and upwards
to the sky. I still see the flowers
as we run around, dressed
in yellow shirts as if dancing
along with our song.

My mother sees
my brother
grab your leg
and throw the bat.
He wants to hit the moon.
I still see the cars
drive by when the sun
has gone down.

Everybody in the street
is there. The smiling kids
searching for one more night
and one more night
to feel alive. You reach
to hold me. You whisper 'ok,'
you cry 'ok,' you whisper 'ok,'
you ask 'ok,' 'ok,' and 'ok,'
'ok,' and 'ok,' you wonder 'ok,'

and 'ok,' you think 'ok,'
you hold my hand and say 'ok,'
you lie there on the grass,
the stars show through your tears,
and 'ok,' you lie there
like you've done every night.
And it's ok.

THE HYPOCHONDRIAC

I've killed my own hands by
placing them under a hot kettle
and held the spout
for about half an hour. It was
the worst torture and the best
punishment, for not as
wounded as the kettle as you'd
expect from the steam, the
burning of the palms is
so intense
that the pain becomes
transfigura-
tion, and I felt more than one
miracle in the burning and
the red blood
in one motion.

BIG BEAR'S WARTIME FARM HEROES

There are two villages.
One is behind you.
Another is here.
They don't
talk to each other.
We are not allowed
to say their names.
I love the cold
and the snow.
I love the
night.
I love the
fire in the night.
I can't live
inside this town
anymore.

I am
the only one who doesn't
feel
the ache in our collective chest.
I can hear the whispers
of the one I call Father
and think of
the rocks
in your hand.
I am your hyena.
It's I, the heat
on your ribs.

It's I, the heat
on your legs.
It's I, the heat
on your hands.
It's I, the pain.

THE FLESH EATING BIONIC SQUIRREL

The words are simple, the tone is moving
like a surrealist sculpting rain
as I take a picture of the pink petals
the carriageway loves so dearly.

My brain is magnetized
to The Strokes' sound
and its stupidity.

Even after I finish,
the song is still spinning in
my head, and I have
no words to speak.

>*my voice has gone into*
>*quiet mode and we are left*
>*to shuffle out of this*
>*mind together like friendly foxes*

You don't exist
>*the fable repeats itself*
Because you are DEAD.

The town, the nondescript little
boy next door,
hides in the woods.

Our teachers are dead.
I am alive.

MUFFIN MCWORMS

The first time a candle went out on its own
I screamed out of sheer fear,
it doesn't explode the way the book says it will–
it gives a gust of black smoke like its own expression.
I hate all the rules about open caskets
especially if you plan on donating
what's inside the casket to science.
I wish I could eat a cannonball whole
and chew at its underbelly like a newt
until its ribs crack and all you see
is yellow lemon-peel pulp.
I don't know if that would bring me
back to life, but that's what I've always wanted.

HONEY BADGER

The sea and the sky are all we have
and what is ours is yours.
I wish that I could fall into a lake of oil,
so you can pull me out with a rope made of seaweed.
I wish you could find the words
to tell the police that your mother and I
fell off a bridge in two separate planes of existence.
I wish you could find the words
to say I was born in the wrong town.
I wish you could find the words
for when the whole world thinks that you are dying,
but you aren't.
I wish you could see how this will all go wrong.

When you're ready to die
and the fire comes for your heart,
ask for two things:
>ask for the moon
>and then ask for it all.

SONG OF THE DAWN

Everything has been twirled around
and around by language, frothed like angry dogs
until the island which gave life froze in imitation
of a big head. Many a moon the sides of the head
have crusted like fortresses upon an outpost.
It is unfashionable. We, alone, jump
in every drivable vehicle chasing
a tornado's body weighing options up at the dry cleaners.
I regret I have never drowned a water-splashed fire truck
and laughed briefly while snuffing out life
and provided you a baby pool to cry around.
The tar beads are full of soap, and you tell me I am smart,
you tell me I am a selfish, godless hypocrite.
You say you've never heard a poem as bad as this one,
yet you only throw critiques because it saddens me,
disgusts you, relieves you from the guilt
of a drive-by shooting. I am not sorry for you,
but I apologise sincerely to my thesis of mechanics.

SONG OF THE MORNING

From cockeyed battlegrounds where raised fists dip
round in awful moonflair, rose flushed skirt
my basketball beard floors on psychedelic shore,
where fingertips dislodged linkages
of space-time linearity and care
for contingency on horizonology
for uneaten or safe skull bruises.
So much rotting slops. Despite sacred protocols
received without a doorway, threshold,
throughout miracle machines offers benediction.
One hails, the others have settled
they label four constituencies
more united by nexus
than atom is on decay
As exit week of nonsense
writers felling reach through shady woodland,
swinging hands displaying
hand-painted earrings,
a member of Poetry plucks tar beads
from our ears and whatever voice
does cause my resolve to broaden
Some soul matters dove on pavement
throws all bare and fearless bleeding itself
taps air mail mark, crunches plucked eyeballs,
murders car.

THE SIDE OF THE POOL

I think I may have fallen
out of a cloud, because
I look like a cloud I feel
like a cloud, and sometimes
I can hear a song coming
from the clouds.

I'm an invisible wind myself,
I just blow across the road
but when the wind is still
I feel like the grass growing, I feel
like the sun, I feel like the bird
with the heartbroken sound.

I can listen, I can hear the noise,
how beautiful it is when rain
comes down. When I was
just a wind there is a bird
that sang and it sang of things
no one else knew.

DAILY FABLES

Dawn disintegrates –
this church's pain and mystery.
Which seems like madness
to ponder everything and hide nothing,
turn heads with acid details, worry
about decorum in two, wear
wild faces to the choir loft.

To venture in this silence, seek
the 'ritual/real/inner'
truths with new allegiance.
Let an echo join you to the old faithful, all
mistrust to brotherhood, opening
crazy night by day,
armies stand solemn, windows open,
challenge world on its way.

The ringing of bells last
left-sided divine joke.
Or was that noise the song
of cantankerous bass-and-horns.
Could another art
be discovered in sounds whose spectrum
blazes upside-down.

Let everybody dance.
The geocentric story:
Pan much too tall got large days, warped
round sun bend to East making ships
ask to see if the old sea-god is not there,

and not answered acceptably open air
with caves drifted through rock might swing out to
find caverns like well get lost and leave.

BIG JOE & THE CAVE OF BONES

Cloud, closer and not well enough known:
following ship of seven wonders (as in needle for mathematics)
tethered to find crown-jewel, giving tools
and worship of sea-god,
empowered by corn-fields, and pilgrims
seeking wise man's wisdom.
Sometimes it's you, and it's not.
Particle-mass of that message in
that noise the voice over:
just want to fix this broken world,
let alone looking
around to find who
makes the noise I make.
Secret texts of a crazy well-told story
they don't quite understand.

The field is blowing, pointing north deeper in echo, connecting the eye to the flood in sun as beyond the sun is the west. Louder and louder and so the promise of the great hell against the wind-tunnel rolling across fields becoming arrows finding their place in the night, one year's worth of memory and fire gathered under the leaves and the trees which no longer step forward into the light.

Everyday man: bathetic, syntheses,
stooping at and of the tiny water-burst.
Perplexing ripples act like a story.
It's an album of yellow, mottled
found rock like a mistake from sunrise to midnight
and finds new words to be words that fit.

As a worm there comes a time
where you know yourself
from within your own light.
Something inside knows all that has happened.
I'm right there, dreaming away
on other things not to move an inch.
I am feeling myself the worm,
watching myself move through the dark,
and cannot resist to laugh
at myself.

It is evening as it has been noon, and noon as it was the day, and the day before it, and before that the evening, and so on, and has been, from the beginning, all before me. The threads of my time fly out of my head and this doesn't matter, and the dreamers on the platform are still perfect.

Open the window, I got to get my breath.
Maybe you do not have to move an inch.
These small things become
all things.
As I show you the beatitudes
you don't believe
but when I speak of you, you want to die
but are not afraid of death.
I want to say you're nothing.
And when your attention
is about you,
the sky will spread its eyelids.
Take off the ideas,
and listen to what has happened inside.
Get somewhere new

and do not be still.
A voice from within you,
gets louder and stronger and louder and louder
and you can no longer sleep.
The eyes and the feet and the feet
I see moving as if in some sort of dance
if you don't move your eyes away from them.
The space that was here is not here,
and it's taking you by the arm,
carrying you to something new.

What's not yet all here is all gone. Let us go. The eye sees all, all of us dancing together, on the night we cannot know, except that we do. Let us go.

I have three sonnets for you,
from three different parts of my life,
each one counting the opposite of each other,
resembling half-time, and counting the other half.
We are made with half and whole,
divided and indivision.
I remember.
My two sons.
One watching.
The other practicing.
I see them dance around me.
I see a split in my soul
that splits itself and multiplies,
on and on
never listening, never pausing,
flying between two realms
feeling some breathing space
and burning all the night away.

JOHNNY 5 FINGERS

they moved
away
from the beach
that they lived on
that they used to spend
the winter and spring on,
that they used to see
the walkers
and the people walking
before all they
could see
were the boats coming,
the boats
on the dark
waters of the harbour
and at first
they liked
what they saw,
they made the best of
the situation,
learnt to love the way that
the changing
shapes were visible
in the dark night
of the harbour,
because there were
some shapes they were familiar
with and for an instant thought

may be the same nuthatch
that they saw the previous year,
resting on the boat they used to sit on,
see the world,
spend the winter
upon the waves
that birthed them.
Now they only see boats,
the whiteness
of the boats,
and they
hear the sound of the
water,
swollen now
by the incoming tide.
They make a habit
of strolling
there now,
floating on these waters and
sailing
down to the
farthest reaches
of the harbour
now merely visitors
in this world
that is somewhere else.

SUPERMAN'S BLACKOUT

I imagine you could take a rock
and twist it into nothing,
like punching someone
in the side of the head
and not even hearing a sound.

THE MAGNETIC FIELDS AT ZERO GRAVITY

Now that was real life I remember.
The words of my childhood.
But no one was there to see me.
No one ever had the pleasure of seeing my soul dance again.
I think there's another world,
where I hear the voices of those who knew me
and those who never tried to get close
and that it all matters.
And I think my soul doesn't know the difference.
It still sounds and feels the same
even as they change.
I go from one to the other
while we still
can't remember
which
is which
the moment and forever in between.

KAIJU NIGHTMARE

I was a beautiful boy.
But even the most beautiful
of beautiful things are also rotten
like all things. It's not really beauty.

Everything will fall. When it does
people will wonder if it ever mattered.
But it always did matter, we just didn't
know it until things changed.

It might have made our time easier,
maybe it was too slow, but in some way
I remember it, even if you forgot
that someday I will die.

Then everything will be
more beautiful than I ever felt before,
like this moment stretched across
eternity's gentle posture.

Everything will go on as the sun
will be the sun will still be coming out
behind them, and it will see them
because we no longer will.

One day you will find that it takes
no part of time but that it is all
of time all at once like a dream
you can't wait to end.

CRONUS (HOME OF THE SOLDIERS)

A member of the mafia always told me that your fortune is written in tinfoil but it doesn't stick unless you bat it against the white wall to get the sharp bark that's inside.

Living alone in your room will surely lead to death.

My whole house smells like ashes.

The faces of all the deceased I have neglected– I should have considered that they would be upset.

When the minutes turned to hours, the hours turned to days.

The second time a candle went out on its own, I didn't even notice.

When the candle was right next to me, I was too busy picking up broken school teacher's portraits that I was sweeping the main room.

And I let it burn forever in there.

This won't do.

Now I have two cats instead of one.

My imagination is gone.

I just let too many movie geniuses kill me.

My only friend opened up her mouth.

The words rolled out of her.

Where have I been all of my years?

I took pictures.

I wanted to stop dead-camera-still.

I need stories that lie on the blank screen, confessional-mode lens.

Much like a deflated balloon, I no longer live.

Write one thousand words of torture tolerance form from composing in any key.

The light bent over the skeletal trees like a skeleton wrist massaged again and again, as a male supermodel concealed it from the light.

Over the madness that emanates from his land a solemn protest urging the public to excuse its condescension.

I am hungry for some spiced popcorn and candy from the stacks of Smith's.

The fruit crusher is my key to fucking up any movie, movie to movie, they change the words to their shit just to get publicity for John Waters' movie 'Serial Mom'.

I BEBOP

We dance on mud they shout
mocking noise behind us
there's people burning
we carry sizzling hearths on our backs
caged men swim timid and peaceful
between arms
feed beasts fat cigars
is there anything nearer pain
than ash from a fitful fire
a puncture wound in my universe
our circumferences are boundaries
across time
back out or back inside
When you grow inside of yourself
between anxiety and ego
when they shove your head
out an exit a sky wide and gape
between limbs I imagine you were forever there
100 long years of a life I abandoned
in a flat roar that demands
an outer cube
And then I shackle myself and padlock my door
with weighted chains
no music crashes through the ceiling
no words bang clot warm
and leave hot waves of sonic black

SCARAMOUCH KAZOO

Give us something to burn.
You awake at dawn but all
you hear is the neighbour
taking down the grass early.

I consider saying, drunk:
I walked into Blackpool once.
Everything on display so fertile.
I got as drunk as anybody.

But later sober I opened the blinds
and saw myself lying on pavement,
cheek by jowl with buckets
and torches, lemons packed in socks.

And it started me off, living
on twigs and shawls.
Enough street energy is
already there when it comes.

Instead I dissociate until I feel like
counting out blind spasms, like
praying to a clenched mouth with claws.
Goodnight my friend, hi Father, yo mother...

CAPTAIN KITTEN

From Ashes:
Empty chasms,
sweeping horizons

Make wisdom
reverse their route
on slow boats to shore.

The dark frozen
flesh of earth crumbles
now as clay does again,

when iron and sand
sift off to transform tiny
angles in all seen paths.

Some ostrich, meanwhile,
does weep for existence,
does contemplate the limp rabbit.

Snow topped steep
banks running aground
for nothing in winter.

In a pile he sleeps
under a peak he
knows as a drop.

Risk decay while
erect he flows
and fields ebb.

As life deep air springs
up, blue pops over
his words, sleet thumping.

Ferocious wings sliced
around the curve-burst
through a gate they did not make.

Burn the men
who live only by fear
and failure to talk.

IT'S HARD TO BE HAPPY AS A BOHEMIAN

Animated like I've eaten my own soul
like I've sewn a voice
into a tongue
cram it down inside my flesh
gourd, deflate like a balloon.
My sentence works like the ventricles
I see my lungs
as a long inflammation
throbbing like heart
lung, no wheeze, no cracks,
use whatever cloth you choose
in the tome,
use whatever filters you've heard.
My final outbreak this morning
when I emptied a deflated lung
into an onerous press,
punctuated the rite of creation,
both a heady ritual,
and the highest hell, as you've said.
I'm pleased that I was unable to show
that plea to the censor
or say that this, it is my last
... this is what I can do
I'll end my possession
of this bronchi
I wish to call
my mother.
The Gramophone

The same question, over and over,
you answer onerously
teaching me to recite the answer
a piquant lesson in writing
patience of fire
and pagination.

THE ROCKONS
AKA Reasons to Stay Alive

1. Well, I say it's overgrown,
a stairway to Nowhere.

2. It's a ridiculous study,
a fantasy toadstool
in the middle of the ward
where no one sees it.

3. Please give it back.

4. Let's have more of that
awful music

5. We're having a test
to see if your heart still beats.

6. I'm sorry,
but I have a bit of an
end-of-semester headache.

7. Excuse me,
that's your consolation.

8. I've been ruined by
the pigeons and the rats.

9. Well, it's my crime
to be the only man
and woman,
jigsaw in hand,
standing in
the underground
garden.

10. It's too small
for me, I'll
never fit in
it, it's full of air
and egg-laying
dung and dust.

11. If I were to be a body,
I think I'd be
half baguette
and half brain.

12. In the hospital
they always try to
turn me away.

13. Do I look dead
to you?

14. Look, I'm right here.

15. They're going to burn
me alive.

16. I'm really quite lazy,
and just not interested in
sheet music.

17. I'll be reversing.

18. We really do have a test
tomorrow.

19. When I see him,
I'm going to give
him to you.

20. There's no point
in running, you'll just
end up being a turtle,
sheltered away in a corner.

21. I'm serious
about my fascination.

22. I have a bat in my car.

23. I think I'll stay a little longer.

24. I will. I won't
leave until you let me.

25. Let's go on a picnic.

26. I want to talk.

27. I will.

28. Please don't do this.

29. This is my future.

30. This is our destiny.

31. I think I'll go to
the chapel
for a while.

32. It's a one-way ticket.

33. Would you mind
bouncing off me for a while?

34. I think I'll find
my own place.

35. That's a tricky situation.

36. There's nothing to
the other side,
it was all a dream.

37. I'll be back as soon
as I'm reanimated.

38. So far there's not
a sign
of my body.

39. Cool, you can see
everything and
no one gets hurt.

40. Why don't you come back?
Why?
Some Days are Harder
I heard you say
I want you to have
a plan
from now on.

41. O, in my dreams
all the shops
come alive
and
you're there,
with me
around
the corner.

THE NEW GAMBIT / THE KOALABAT

After I was born I was carried up to heaven
by angels who hung me in a doorway.
You were already there, playing the Koala
by yourself. I am not your brother,
you will never like me the way I am.

Write some poems, write a book,
numbers don't count. Now I am
born in the night into a world of midnight.
I am a sentinel, a shepherd. I exist
because it was nice of you to ask me to exist.

We had a chance, I never got it back.
This is an exorcism.

THE LIGHTNING KLAXON RIDING SHOTGUN

I'm a moth on a gauze curtain
in a state of advanced decay
but I'm alive.

I accept the fact of death and birth
because all living is built upon dust
and gold—ceremonial gifts of life.

I wish it didn't have to be this way.
But I know it is and I accept it.
You are one of the young who came before us—

this window we're looking out of.

OLD ROW REDUX

original instruments of communion
analogous flamenco then there are
velociraptors
to the tribe of first kinfolk
all terrain nothing more
close or far was no-thing
everything was doomed to
remain we climbed every mountain
downhill everyone following up
blindfolded the deer oh-so-casual
others pursued with ever more-haughty determination
hemlock or blood
or whatever
Eon, seagulls, kraken --
clouds, thunderous, tortuous waves --
our lost form rang out into lonely oblivion
became palimpsest with some other
reflectorising impulse
within contact
through these acts we join up in a cloud
image-sense's dusk-to-dawn -disposition
and uncover fundamental
structure
if we suppose a God
a field of historical memory
then concurrency is merely fated to
be notary: text so goes the law
one's way of dealing with the past is to do so

piously if possibly in an excess
or however we recall it
what if in terms of free association or retroactive
embroidery of redemption by contrast...
accomplishments in the order of psychic contents
exceed expectations
and by this amount
in expressing the dialectical
it gives a contradictory simplicity of inner truth
a two-level charm of the possible opposite
a revolution in understanding
in an integration of the gaps
that we fall into how else are we to understand
how can anyone be certain
that he isn't the enemy?
for instance treachery becomes consolation
murder the destruction of a common good
symbolised in the moment of metaphor.
and the words are intelligible
if we accept that they are their own elements
and the glyph is as natural
as the division line
a necessary acknowledgement
of a reality beyond meaning
we are living within an anomic
dynamo
of common value
discovering where we belong
(clandestinely)
a pre-state collective pursuit

of that illusory wisdom
realising its immense power
(or consuming its concrete)

WELL-FERMENTED CRUST

We, my friend, we sing songs
about fires in the sky,
even though music scares me;
those synthesizer beats
keep the lights on when the music
gives me chills and night turns
to day without you. When you left
the house was a music video
that inspired a song. Your resonance
made the walls ring and scream.

I wish you could have tried harder
to make it all more real. I wish
I could take away the many possibilities
that were lost with your imperfect gift.
Every river and stream overflows
when I let it. We both know that if
I hit you with the finger of fury,
you will simply become a puddle.

I wish I could see how to let you go,
so I could help you fly, fly like a pigeon
that is falling to its death, flying
on broken wings with reckless abandon.

I wish I could watch the sun set, see
the fire that makes you laugh, the fire
that makes you cry; instead I watch
the greying sky become less full of stars.

BOBBY STUBBS AND THE LONG HORNS

prying open and tracing the threads
in front of the kin
willing to share
us for but a glimmer
we'll never learn where
to look but we'll never stop
it does not matter if we should die
this is a convergence
of the Imaginary state
and the Informal use of language
revenues -- let them
love their memories
a babbling self-editing
where the vernacular wiles
cannot undo (shall not)
but...reward
and pay the piper
when this is all done...
we are all that's left
of this universe
all of us in the choirs of one
and the truth is out there
waiting for the interpreters
with a notation.

O GALILEO WHERE ART THOU SATELLITES

Yet I feel the dance in your light and movement or
my feel that you feel it. We both may spin but
the stars spin and no stars may spin as they spin in space
Yet you dance with me yet we are as one:
and you that feel we have no place in this space
and so as all our place and the feel we are moving
we dance with one another moving only when we want to.
So the stars spin and we are dancing now
but dancing and dancing in the dark in what may
become night in the next century but never dark,
dark only until time and then there is light
and the stars are dancing may it be with us in
each other when time becomes light,
where Earth, a satellite, spins in orbit
around the central sun, like a tiny pebble
on the rim of a vast, decadent waterfall.
Where you orbit around me our life cycles
are measured, the orbits made tighter,
And I, from orbit through Earth orbit.
You are a star in a galaxy of stars and a galaxy of stars.
The moon would rather not be here
any more than you, fodder for poets.
As you step, so you dance, and when you dance,
others dance. You feel your relative steps
and so there is motion. The Moon moves.
The Sun moves, and the Pleiades move you,
their constellations steady as pendulums.

THREE EIGHT SONGS

Blood ties like
longer chromosomes;
Some people burn
a piece of landscape,
splashing water on it.
But not me; I grow
a forest where no trees grow
and rub out the clouds.

I see the lakes,
from on high.
The water has changed
colour; I try
to remember
what it used to be,
I try to remember
the colour blue.

I am at the edge
of my consciousness.
I've waited long for this;
it is my first poem
about poetry.
Into that sun,
it must shine,
and it does.

MR. KITE'S WORSTED

I.

I have a garden with strawberries.
Here's my garden full of petals.
I need another garden.
I was so lonely I lost my shadow
but it's my shadow, it's inside
the sun. Where did you put
my shadow? I'll find it,
then it won't be sad.
Each plant needs to grow
in a different direction.
Green on the left is a day,
red on the right is a dawn

II.

The rain is mad, but the rain
never knows how to speak.
Like a lap dog it watches everything.
The way it looks at you, you can't see
it, it's invisible, but it's right there.
This is my garden, it's round like
sun, it's strong like wheel.
If you can hold on to the green plants,
you'll be home at long last.

III.

We said *the rain is so mad*
but the rain said *i love you*
and on that day we talked about where
rain would go after it had done what
it had to do. There were some flowers,
some orange, but they all grew together
to make one beautiful sky.
Where does the sky go, after the rain?

IV.

We watched as the rain went
through our bedroom window.
It went into her sock drawer, then out again.
This is my garden, you can climb it
but you must be careful,
you can't make holes in it.

V.

My garden fits in a suitcase.
I pick the flowers when you are sad.
And when you are sleeping
I pick a few more for me.

3 SEASONS OF THE O. C.

Something mysterious
in the marine
environment, maybe.
We could write that down.
Tectonic movement, yes
perhaps massive flooding, death,
or decay, yes.

The skeleton, that seems to fit,
but what if the skeleton is a person?
For all we know, it could be a living person.
That's exciting.
It could be a living, breathing person.
It might be your dead girlfriend.
How romantic. How peculiar.

Was that her mother peering through the window?
Does she know your wife is in the room?
Is she mortified? Is she lonely?
The horror of it all.

There is an upside to this.
If you were still alive, you never would have known misery.
You never would have bought a seat on this ship.
You wouldn't have dated the ocean floor.

There is no downside to this.

FREDDY VS JASON VII: FLOWER DRUM SONG

I've always been fascinated by the way words
and meanings change over time.

As they travel
with those traveling
to the edge
of all language.

How many times a word
has been used
to mean all different things.

It used to refer to the body.

The body of the earth, the body of a living person.

People's bodies,
plants, animals,
the earth,

Then they came to mean:
The planet.
The sun.
The moon.
The entire solar system.

Then words changed
in what they meant.

And changed the meaning
of the word.

It went from
meaning the thing
that we are made of
to meaning the thing
that our existence depends on.

So, when you say the word earth
you are not quite understanding
what it means.

I.M. JONATHAN LIVINGSTON SEAGULL

The first time we came down,
I sat in bed beside a dead bird
and I was really worried.

A whole new language of words
I'd never thought to notice.
I didn't know they were in the house.
One called me "baby."
One called me "father."
One called me "sister."
One called me "mother."

We all shared the same word "mother."
We all shared the same word "water."
We all shared the same, small world.
We all shared,
a broken bird
in our house.

A whole new language of words
I'd never thought to notice.
I didn't know they were in the house.
One called me "baby."
One called me "father."
One called me "sister."
One called me "mother."

We all shared the same word "mother."
We all shared the same word "water."
We all shared the same, small world.

We all shared,
a dead bird
in our house.

A house with a broken house.
A house with a broken bird
in our house.

JENŐ'S GHOST, THE UNFINISHED SYMPATHY

I was in my bed,
and I felt like
someone was there.
I closed my eyes
but it was still there
even with my eyes closed.
So I opened my eyes.
It was the sun
coming through my window.
It was the sun that I saw
before I was born.

I was alone on the beach
and everything turned
into a picture.
Everything came together
in my brain and
I could see
everything around me.

The moon, it rose out
of a lake. The waves
moved the moon.
It turned into a cloud
and left my mind.
The clouds left the moon
and the moon left my eyes.

THE ENDLESS EXPLODING LIGHTS

Misery writes poems for breakfast,
then each shovel with fist
flesh to soil, twine rope into pen,
misery severs a spinal cord.
Poetry comes, brings forth its house pet,
stuck crust of scavenger mind,
elephantine great belly.
Words, clumsy as birth, the text
drops wet into an open mouth.
No quick, well chosen, pause,
acrobatic space to cast off,
for poets feasting in unhinged morass,
wetting the mouth without embarrassment,
unscrupulous in food and syrup,
like rats in a maze chewing without restraint
poetic voice gets purged
then meanders back down the corridor,
bleeding towards the molten fountain,
turning around when the elephant roars,
before lumbering back towards the cave.

THE MILLIONAIRE FIRE FIGHT

Every public house I have lived in,
is now a tear-gas range
for those left against a wall.
Since we moved to the green state
there has not been an apartment free of scorpions
or mice, lurking in corners.
Cheap wine, canned goods
old food for seven hundred years
remains over time on shelf.
Dark secrets, fear.
Poetry, and poetry alone,
should always drink water.
Moonstruck, river gazer, loves those
who are vulnerable, those who are lonely,
poets who look through cracked windows
those who must walk the city or die.
soul spatters into puddles, dries hard,
then joins reflection, next to the skull, to await restoration.
I like writing with you
Because our eyes have not touched,
like the barest breaths of lovers
I cannot know if you know I love you
so, so very much
and who I was and who I'm trying to be
like no-one else, so too, will be no-one else.
Your vision like tincture of night,
fluctuating, striking out, then
you deliver with pointed palm
the rite that emerges from the shaft of gloom.

WOLFPACK BEATS PER MINUTE

Words clear nothing
then bleed on
enchantment flows
to myth from vernacular
drones which feed on a destructive
feel it, love, haunt everything:
borders, scenery, landscape,
but taste it, taste it
when you breathe in, taste
what have you left behind
the steam from the kettle,
the city on a hill,
those books in the library
I forgot to read for an assignment
that never happened,
what else does this language fail to answer
the horizon of a hidden face
under stalks,
with quiet answers
to questions I should never ask
make me hear you
just between us.

HIGH TECH MADNESS

I know the moon was blue once
before it stopped being blue.
I know the sky's colour changes.

I don't know where the moon goes
or how the trees are when no one is around
except for a bird or two waiting
to have their nests repaired.

The moon moves in a silent direction,
I watch it go and think about if it was
once blue and where it goes when it
isn't blue anymore. I never saw the sun
or the sky. My mind has pictures of them
so that I can believe in all the things I know.

YOU KILLED MY COUSIN IN A DRIVE-BY

A piece of herself
hurled into a mausoleum.
There were no children in that town.
All were dead. All were gone.

When she died all the children
were stillborn. In the house
the dead children cried
because of the death
of my cousin. The funeral
had been too late
to bury her soul.

I feel her like the breath
of a child in the still room
of the world. A hole
in the earth for a time.

She was still part of
the world and she lived
on after the funeral
but her face had become
an emblem of
the human struggle.

THE ROAD TO WRESTLEMANIA

You go on, I'm not there
I was once but now I'm something
else that I can't name but
it's a thing I have been, a thing
I still am and it never goes away,
my own kind of ghost, my own
kind of death. My death
was never really about death
it was about the end of
being me in the way I was
the way I lived. It was like
a fire, it was like a flood, it was like
a stroke, it was like a war
and it was like an accident
and it was like a fight
and it was like a storm, it was
like a hurricane and it was
like a hurricane and it was
like a hurricane and it was
like a hurricane and it was
like a hurricane and it was
like a hurricane and it

ANGRY HIPSTER ON ACID

When I woke I was sitting on the church roof at night eating clams, having put cigarettes out on my own eyes while I slept. Somebody below was chipping away at headstones with crooked teeth. I would've filmed it but while I was dying all the lens from my super 8 cameras were stolen by a 6 feet old man made of superglued fingers. It was late but an unknown entity was violently murdering the local Catholic priests, before poisoning egrets with factory farmed petroleum. When I crept back to the hospital, one of the baristas was squabbling with the another. I shouted shit, just pour the drink and move on. I return to the ICU to the raucous sound of canned laughter from 80s sitcoms, but nobody brought a steady procession of Wild Things like I was promised. My ice cream money had been stolen, and a middle-aged woman with the name tag 'Buffy' had followed me back. She reliably informed me that she is the one who causes the entire town, every so often, to wake up at night sweating. I out salt and pepper in the fridge, the pantry, the microwave, and the coffee pot, and set a reminder to go to the supermarket to look for my house key. When I finally fell back into my deathbed, the nurses began updating me every hour, if not more frequently, with what was happening on BBC Two. I watched an allusion to someone called Bill Shakespeare try to stab God, and run to the kitchen. He died of carbon monoxide poisoning. I went to bed, in an old man's sleep, with the feeling I was a show home waiting to be erected. I was never awake, merely dreaming in alliteration.

BRAINS 'N' CAKE

Some people said that the dead can't get sick,
and that if they die they die a clean death.
But then I saw a man in hospital,
his heart having been damaged so badly,
that it burst, and then began to calcify inside him.

My wife's sister told me she had become a cannibal,
if I did not find a way to stop her, she would eat my heart.
I woke from a deep sleep, and saw that the clock read 1400,
my wife had been sitting on the floor with her face in the corner
for the last 6 months.

> *My wife's sister has become a cannibal.*
> *The cannibal wants my heart for breakfast.*
> *I must get my wife to stop it before it gets her.*
> *I must go now, a stranger is waiting at the front door.*

He wants to buy my house. He wanted to buy
the house in the beginning, but I refused.
When the house was vacant, I was not home,
or else he would not have gotten inside.

He was asking where the garden was.
He seemed to think that I had a garden. He is a stranger.
I could have asked who he was, but I could not bring myself
to speak, or move, or move my mouth to speak.

He went in and pulled an old girl out.
The old girl looked familiar,
but there is no garden,
there is no old girl. Just my wife's sister
digesting my salted heart.

WAITING FOR THE SHOW TO GO ON

There is a face in the water.
The face laughs.
I go back to bed wearing one sock and no pants.
My bed is filled with penguins.
There is no rain today.
Today is a sunny day.
There is no snow.
Tomorrow it will rain.
I'll listen.
They'll see the rain.
It will melt the snow.
It will become ocean.
Penguins join in the ocean.
I will try to be part of the ocean.
I will stare into it.
I will sing.
I will dance.
I will forget about the murderers who killed me.
Freckles! Freckles!

I SELDOM PRAY TO RABIES

It's hard to walk down the street
when you've got rabies.
I had it when I was a kitten.
I was near some kittens
and some of them bit me,
I got a broken tooth and a bad gash

and some of the blokes I lived with
called me Yoda after Star Wars,
I didn't know what that was,
they just called me Yoda
so I just smiled and stared.

It's like with books
I never read one that got away.
Some people have gone missing
while reading a book.
Some animals never learned to bark.

I can still remember a scene,
that scene is still on my mind
but it's no longer there,
a book now is only a hole in my head,
like a picture torn out of a diary.
I like to think I killed that book,

but that's impossible
because the book is dead.

There was nothing living inside it.
It was a blank book with blank pages.

The very best part of you,
is the part you don't show,
a creature you hate.

NAVAL

The room is lit by stars.

A dog is barking far.
A cat sits purring by

on my bedside, I hear
noise of traffic in the street.
I smell the rain
outside my house.

There's something I should do,
I feel it's something you should've known

the night before.
In the light of morning
all that had seemed dark,
fading with the morning.
Gathered at my kitchen table
my friend was a new friend
I was glad, I'd never been happy.

We were happy, I was with him, my best friend.
He brought me to my old house,
he took me to my old house,
we drank a pint of whiskey,
he smoked a spliff.

We listened to Bach; and my friend
was talking about his cat.

His cat had been running loose
every night for years.
Now that he's a grown man
it's the first thing he thinks of
when his wife goes out for the day.

ADVENTURES OF THE UPSIDE-DOWN BOYS

I will tell you about the things I can remember.
The sky always looks very different
when you're flying, it feels like you can reach out
and touch it. I'm lying next to you on the sofa.
The sofa and you are both dirty. The house is a mess.
I wish you were here. There are many things I want to tell you,
but it is hard. I think it would be better if we were sitting
together again, talking in my room. We should have left,

but we didn't know. Do you remember when we went outside
to look for the key? It looked like we were outside forever.
I wanted to go back inside, but there was only you.
Where we came from seemed so much smaller. My father
wanted to talk to my mother but she couldn't understand
what he was saying. It was too loud, then he fell over.
My sister saw me trying to help him but she screamed.
There was blood on the floor. I was too scared to help my father.

I heard the front door slam. I ran out of the house
and was in the park. I started walking. I wanted to look
for someone to save my mother. I wanted to get help
for my father. I wanted to bring my mother back home,
but there was nobody there, just some old buildings.
I saw a train that was about to leave, but it didn't leave.
A long red train, maybe a ferry, but it wasn't moving,
just slowly moving in a circle. I was so cold and scared

and I couldn't move, my legs were heavy. It was hard
to feel my feet. It was so cold, and I couldn't understand
what was going on. I started to cry. I didn't know what to do.
I didn't know what I was supposed to do. I started to shake.
I kept shaking. I remembered being in the park with my mother,
in front of the ice-cream kiosk, before the park. I don't know
why I didn't run away. Maybe I thought the noise was a game.
It was dark outside, but the lights were on inside the kiosk.

I didn't want to go back inside. It was too bright. The smell
of ice cream. I wanted to go to the train station,
but it didn't exist. I started to run. I was running
with all my strength. I heard a man calling my name.
I was running, and it was so dark. It was so dark.
I didn't know where I was running to.

BEETHOVEN'S THIRTEEN HUNDREDTH

I have a friend who cut her finger, and the flesh kept falling off. I have a friend who once shaved a cat in my bathroom and accidentally shaved the bathtub. I have a friend who once dropped a glass of water on a cobra and killed it. I have a friend who caught a water moccasin with his bare hands. I have a friend who ate a live shoe. I had a friend who swallowed a live scorpion. I had a friend who ate a plastic bag full of dirt and grass and she went into convulsions and died. I have a friend who drowned in a puddle of water and tried to find his way out by digging. I have a friend who touched his brother's mouth and he choked to death. I have a friend who drank paint thinner in a bathtub. I have a friend who got on a plane to nowhere to kill some people and then he was killed. I have a friend who tied a big stick to a pig's tail and it hit him in the nose and broke his nose. I have a friend who made a jellyfish sandwich and ate it. I have a friend who was a Navy Seal and he slept with the commandant of his course. I have a friend who hired a male prostitute who dressed in a spider monkey suit to drag him behind a truck. I have a friend who stole a pencil and wrote the word "LOVE" on a wall with it. I have a friend who got two peyote cacti and ate them. I have a friend who stuffed dry leaves into her body and she went crazy. I have a friend who fell in love with a tree. I have a friend who cut off his own balls and made a necklace out of them. I have a friend who dressed in a bumble bee suit and tried to seduce a train. I have a friend who looked at her blood-drenched hand in the hospital and said, "Well, I guess I'm a murderer." I have a friend who studied the Swiss forest masters to improve her game of pool. I have a friend who mowed lawns for money. I have a friend who walked up to a convenience store and pushed a bag of dog shit through the cashier's window. I have a friend who told his teacher he was in love with the colour purple. I have a friend who sold postage stamps for a living. I have a friend who taught himself to sew and made a dress out of newspaper. I have a friend who sold pot. I have a friend who made a needlepoint of his face. I have a friend who told a doctor she was having sex with her own head. I have a friend who laughed when her boyfriend lost a goldfish in the toilet. I have a friend who sat down on a tiger's tail and stayed there until the tiger ran away. I have a friend who laughed when she cut herself shaving. I have a friend who put a black magic marker in his ear and it burned a hole in his head. I have a friend who chased a clown down a street. I have a friend who drank a whole bottle of Tylenol and swallowed a razor blade. I have a friend who went to the dentist for a cleaning and was shocked when he saw a baby tooth. I have a friend who ate a glass of water and fainted. I have a friend who threw a penny at a lightning bolt. I have a friend who swallowed a tree branch and broke his neck. I have a friend who swallowed a dead body. I have a friend who inhaled a balloon and passed out. I have a friend who urinated on an electric fence and got shot with a stun gun. I have a friend who ate a bottle of cologne. I have a friend who stuffed newspaper into his ears and then he got a headache. I have a friend who burned his nose and spat blood on a clown. I have a friend who wrote a brief article about himself in the newspaper. I have a friend who owned and managed a successful record store for 20 years. I have a friend who ran a newspaper. I have a friend who wrote a very good book. I have a friend who founded a small company. I have a friend who was stabbed in the neck with an ice pick. I have a friend who banged his head against a brick wall and was in a coma for two days. I have a friend who killed himself with a stapler. I have a friend who put toothpaste in his anus. I have a friend who performed oral sex on a banana. I have a friend who sewed his wife's hair to the waistband of his shorts. I have a friend who mixed his urine with alcohol and drank it. I have a friend who threw a pie at the Pope. I have a friend who set himself on fire in a mall. I have a friend who shit on the top of a moving train. I have a friend who put needles in his eye and didn't notice. I have a friend who used a shoehorn to put her head through a wall. I have a friend who put his head inside a grenade. I have a friend who chewed glass and his mouth and nose were sewn shut. I have a friend who put perfume in his ears and slept with one ear open. I have a friend who pinched his own nipples until they bled. I have a friend who wrote a bad review of the Toronto Symphony Orchestra. I have a friend who gave himself a bath and kept his finger in the water the whole time. I have a friend who bled to death from a paper cut. I have a friend who cut her tongue in half. I have a friend who bought $1.50 worth of gum and put $2.00 worth in her pocket. I have a friend who tried to eat his own hair. I have a friend who tied a knot in his shoelace and got blood poisoning. I have a friend who coughed up a lung. I have a friend who drowned in a fishbowl. I have a friend who sat in a bucket of fish. I have a friend who threw a jar of jam in a river. I have a friend who was swallowed by a whale. I have a friend who froze himself to death in a snowstorm. I have a friend who came out of the ocean with his skin on fire. I have a friend who shot a can off a roof to see if it would fly. I have a friend who had sex with a ghost. I have a friend who set himself on fire to see if he could feel it burn. I have a friend who set his car on fire and tried to crawl through the burning wreckage to safety. I have a friend who ate a cyanide capsule and survived. I have a friend who wanted to be an actor but got stuck in traffic. I have a friend who ate a package of nuts and was only served a second helping. I have a friend who climbed a fountain and drank the water. I have a friend who cut his ear off with a lawnmower and woke up the next day. I have a friend who dug his own grave and suffocated himself in it. I have a friend who built a catapult and wanted to know what it was like to be hit in the testicles by a shot from that catapult. I have a friend who ate a live moth and woke up two days later in a field of yellow daisies. I have a friend who took a pill and threw up in front of a mirror and got a great idea for a new sales strategy. I have a friend who shaved his face and chest in the same sitting. I have a friend who kicked a tree stump and made it explode. I have a friend who put a lit cigarette in her ear and blew it out with a shotgun. I have all these friends and not a single story to tell.

IF YOU THINK THERE IS TOO MUCH SCENT

Taken one step at a time,
so the earth can breathe a little slower too.
But we are all creatures of light and dark.
We know what kind of life
a pine tree can withstand.
This isn't poetry about dead whales,
or polar bears. There is nothing poetic at all
about any animal's being dead for a reason
that has nothing to do with my garden,

The purpose of the Forest of Dead Wood Art Project
is to create the most copies of The Dead Wood Art Project.

A forest is my forest—
my forest of a lifetime—
so no one is going to come
and remove all the trees
in my forest or my forest of life.
I'm sorry you must die.
But you're dead and gone.

We can't stop the process,
but the world, including the forest,
does turn over each second—
it is not a fixed place.

TAKE OUT A GUN AND BLOW OFF YOUR FOOT

I grabbed onto the neck of
a loose dog that had bitten me
once. It didn't seem dangerous,

just a pain in the back of my knee
and a joy at the shock of the
bite, but the owner was furious.

He took me and bit my hand
as if there were little coins
in his mouth.

SECRET TEXTS OF A HORROR STORY

Not being ever found.
        An ocean without a song,
                as sirens laughing
                      as people sacrificed.

Blank, entire field of night.

A cloak where there's light,
        not of joy, of meditation
                free-style
                      My shapeless self

Spills unarticulated life,

for awhile in crystal,
        fastest on the silent
                planet, in blind spot
                      of phone, radio,

soil, granite,

toppings, of seas
        Deepest human not having anything there,
                in bathroom, in trees. A calm place
                      in a snowed-over city, where

snow pelts, a squirrel sleeps in front

of a window
>   under roof, poured
>   and ragged, gray,
>   but no footprints in snow.

Cocksure.

I like the idea of this poem.
>   Let it be yours.
>   smoke snow-ice.
>   Healing powers of slow-dawn

over-bruised skies snowflakes,

colours distant that's
>   my skin. Nothing strange,
>   no stranger than I but snow
>   with sinuses makes me weep.

THERE ALL RIGHT

There's a ghost that's running along the ceiling.
(Take one at random and it's already in the wall)
You've seen this ghost before.
Hate him, love him.
Now he's free.
You've got to remember this.
He is everywhere.
His fingers are clumsily waving over here
(and then it's in your face)
and I'm bleeding (bleeding)
as he leaves me
(and finally)
his name is Hate.
(I just died)
with my hands bleeding.
I'm dead (died)
and there's nothing I can do about it
(I died)
I've seen The Ghost of Hate (killed me)
from the beginning
(death)
the beginning (I died)
What are you gonna do with this life (rotten)
(half-dead) (won't die) (hates me) (dead)?
Ghost (home of the soldiers)
everything about you (both sides)
everything about you (both sides)
everything about you (both sides)
everything about you (both sides)
everything about you (both sides)

STRONG AND TALL AND MISSING

It's not that I want to
give you any comfort
that this was so easily
taken away.
It's not that I want to
betray the empathy that you
shared with me
and the empathy
that it's safe to assume
you're feeling right now.
But I can't deny it
and I can't explain it
and I can't ignore
that you did
tireless work to find me
and that you found me
without putting me through
a gauntlet of tortures
and let's face it
without really giving me much
to believe in.
It's that after
an entire life dedicated
to loving someone,
at least partially
they are done
trying to keep the peace
for their own comfort

and not for mine
and that I can't
keep my breath
to myself.
Please don't call.
I'll be here
pining for you to see
the cold that's now
brewing in my chest
at the sound of your
cold voice.

OUT BACK TO WORTH INTO THE MIND

The air was like a million
and you stood there feeling sick.
You turned and looked down at your
jeans that were all torn apart
from the waist down.

I am a poet and this
Is my work of art.

Your body loved you so you
kissed it all over. You thought
what's a poet for? To make you
and your body feel nothing that
would hurt you as you walk out
from all of us.

That's when I saw the broken
mirror in the house. No one cleaned
it out, and I can feel something coming.
Oh I can't see so much, but I can hear.
There's a pain I can hear and feel
at the same time. I put my hand
inside yours and that's when
you said I must be
a very sad man.

I've been here in this room
bitter from the heart sick soul;
lonely and alone.

I held my ears open, you poured in
your tears—O, such painful hearses.
I can help you with the cabinets
when they start rattling like a ship from
the side of the street going up a hill

Then what you feel I feel all over.

THE LAST NIGHT WAS THE LAST NIGHT NOT THE FIRST

If someone starts screaming,
we might find an ear on the floor.
If they aren't screaming
they probably have the same
dream every time. You can hear
the ocean when there's no electricity.
It's hard to hear it under
all that screaming. It is dark
and you're there under the screaming.
We are all afraid it might happen again.
I wish the ocean was louder. We could
see what it really looks like
if the ocean was yelling louder.
We might just find an ear
on a shelf in an ear museum.
The ear on the end of "the thing"
comes out when you find the thing.
One last ear will keep the thing quiet.

The thing looks so real
that it won't be easy to see it.
It might be one of your grandfathers.
It might be a fish. At least it is
something. But it is made of nothing,
except for that thing. It might be
some kind of boat made
with the most valuable thing.
The boat might not smell right.

You don't usually know
what an ocean smells like
and the ocean doesn't usually feel
like the ocean unless there are waves
on the water. I once saw an eye, it was blue
and I tried it with some sugar water
and I thought it would help but it seemed
to have a mind of its own. It didn't work.
It tried to eat the finger I stabbed
its eye with on an island.

THIS ONE'S TINY FRIEND

My headless body was hanging in the tree.
I couldn't tell if it was a ghost
or a figment of my imagination.
I ran to the grocery store to get an axe.
I thought I could kill the tree.

I came back with a car. The tree fell.
I put my head on a spoon
and ate it by candlelight
and threw up, poisonous.

I put my head on a
B-52 bomber.
I left it in a phone booth
in Dallas, Texas.
There are flying saucers hovering
in the sky, and my head
is on a table at Sydney Opera House.

I'm on the roof.
My head is at sea.

OH GOD I'VE PEAKED!!!

This plate
of nachos
was bought
for the sole

purpose of
eating the
whole fucking
thing. And not

one of you
could possibly
do anything
about it. This

fucking thing
I am eating
is going to
explode in

your goddamn
face. This plate
of nachos, it can
fucking suck

down everything
in the world
and *we love you*.
It would be

a fucking
crime if you
tried to eat
anything else.

DERANGED FUNNY AND SAD

I went into our bathroom
and looked into the mirror
after I had showered and
I just want to know if I can
get my inner child, he must
be only six or seven, out of
my mirror, out of my soul,
and onto the streets.

It's not my problem, that little
kid doesn't care whether he
lives or dies, and I don't give
a damn. Do the world a favour
and let him live.

TRIED TO REMEMBER THE PARTY

If everything is nothing,
just a nothing,
the universe and her heart,
the stars a mirror,
and we can do whatever
as you're standing beside me
all the way. We're going
to the edge and we'll go again.

It might not be your time but
it will be when it wants to be.

Just when it wants to be.

One morning everything will
fall into the empty room of your head;
You will still have your face
as if on a card that you've
sketched it upon.

How will I know if I'm alone
When I'm never alone?

I hope a tree will hold a piece
of you, to fall at night,
to see the moon.

Sometimes a song will come
like a dream that comes like
a song. When all is left is ash
I will go.

BECAUSE MONEY WORKS IN QUEUES

iron lungs pump ounces
of liquid through bare chests
but pale and desperate people
gather round fires set

against money flown into cities
under neon ice; towards promise
rings wear carnations in soles
like the forked toes of cats out

in more creative streets heads
all turn, dares to nod, licks smoke
from braziers without mind in vacant
galleries speculative daisy day

markets buy roses in summer
for jam peppers, wine in saucers
hot in the sunlight—tomorrow
of reform's complaint attracts customers

in ripped gumminess
this street parade redeems umber
sketches but throws locals east-of-beyond
bombs tunes sung tired far south lets

heartstrings black as luminaries
(it told them what violet hills look like,
which tide announced rise and success
strikes the thief lets his guilty private

watch someone starve) lost bravado
from passports vomit less not remind
themselves about trying again letting
bands blast telly has suppressed traces

of sparks (didn't report garden bomb
to Interpol as vital being
no one sleeps with their head
between their knees

except in the arms
of a mother,
a friend,
or a lover

THOSE WHO GOT MUMMIFIED TO BE LEFT ALONE

he's a man who thinks of time as if
to me the trees are of this century.
The one thing you do when you're young
is to think of time.

In my house the cat sits for hours
the same cat who's in the family for ages,
       or at least the same as

in his eyes he found what he was looking for:
a woman with a face like that of a mannequin.

(Let others tell the paradox).

he takes in more or less of the same
all you've been doing this whole while

what it doesn't look like is
the fact that he is on no account to know
 if it is

the trees are of this century.
    and they say
    that the sun goes up into my heart
when all of you do,

The sun doesn't rise up inside you.
Your heart goes up.

the sun doesn't go down in you
and that if you should

If you should

If we're going to see such things
there's a price to pay.

The summer was huge, and hugely gone.
  what happens when
        (i.e., we have the sun
              in our souls
)

a kind of god it will ever be
that's how the world's made to be
but the trees are of this century
for

a kind of god.

LIKE RED SCREAMING FROM HOME

My brothers and I lived in a house
that had been knocked about a bit
and still smelled of the sea, I remember
in our basement the sound of an iron
being dragged across the floor.

The first place you remember—when
I was a boy—for it to be over, when I
could get to the end of the porch and breathe
in. We are the only thing that will never
be over, but I'll let you down now.

> *I believe in everything*
> *that the world stands for...*
> *the idea that anything*
> *at all is not in itself absurd,*
> *and that anything I never wanted*
> *to tell, as I'd never have a reason*
> *to tell it. Everything at once.*

MY ANGRY DAYS

And each one of us have said
our dead are with us and have not died.
They are merely back in the dawn
with sadness, but if you wait,
a little fire extinguishes it.

Just like the things that go, the furniture
is on fire, some nights blizzarded
by hand, time, milk, us gathering
on a leash screaming *flatlines*
and *cigars* from the windows.

THREE STARVING

Show me the road, I said, *any road*. Teach me
a stupid song that wakes me up before
I sleep, and if, one day, you may want
to know how I find myself in the dark
without needing a compass. i know
where I've been. To love is for the living
but the sunshine is sick and I cannot stop it.

 I feel so lost for you are my home,
and therefore we are strangers.
A bit more coffee from the robin
today; I can just about taste it.
We're going with oxygen this weekend.

I have deodorant in my ears
and the mirror wants to touch up its front teeth.
We're going to lie here in the dark
and a beautiful butterfly is going to land
on my mouth. That is how I will know
to expect a quiet night. The same silent burn.

LAST YEAR IS SWIMMING IN A CUP OF BLOOD

We'll all float into the distance,
this could be a full moon after all:
fragile, glacially beautiful.
The poor guy, mining its cheeses
to pay off an old debt. We've noticed
what was left of him and you said
there's something wrong with that sort
of thing, and then you began to laugh.

If you're feeling hard-done-by
interpret these whispers: the TV
may be too big, the blood coffee thicker
than it should be, no off-duty moon
cops to place a pulse on an EKG,
just a robot that sings their blues.

The one-eyed man isn't gone,
he watches you stare out the window
though there is nothing in sight
but the end of that street and his
remaining eye – the eye that is turning,
the eye that is slowly taking on
the shade of a poet who remains absent.

There's only you and there's only
that sightless man, and we're both
going to die one day.

I WILL NOT JUDGE YOU WHEN WE SIT ACROSS FROM EACH OTHER IN THE SILENCE

I could have been just like him, if I'd tried
to love you. I might have given my whole self,
though it would not have been enough.
We loved a little more deeply for it

and that is the way it goes: a sad song
the drowning out of the human voice.
This tells me the earth's future in two things:
the comfort of loving the world, and the doubt

that anything is ever to be perfect, perfect love.
We can never come to an end. It is greater
than everything and exists only in memory,
out of the mouths of those to whom we owe

the tiniest, most contained part of evolution
and exchange the whole for a bag of late nights.
The natural order of things, the ravenous,
craving, compassionate art of art and life.

It is people that we fear, that made us afraid
to enter the bath. I do not wish to believe in God
but sometimes I have to use imperfect logic.
How can I know myself without petals, sweetness,

and hate? An entire belief system may be torn apart,
but I do not know how I got there. It is not just
the words on the page, it is the possibilities
of the wind and my breath in the air around me.

I'M HONESTLY ONLY WRITING BECAUSE I'M SCARED OF WHAT HAPPENS WHEN I DON'T

the difference between being a dog
of a song that keeps my body awake
as the ocean laps and the beaches
sink into your bed to wake up
ive been thinking about the night
when i first opened my ears
when the first
i would die and you
my bones will fall with no trace ill leave no trace
my father once said
when we were lying
we could have saved it
a long distance my heart is always
and the next one
cant wait on any better deal
the second you walk into
the second you come home drunk
we could have used it for lunch
in a time capsule
is the best
and you said we can
the time capsule
is where well come out i guess
i think about having an oblong grave
i think about when i was a child in a dream
the sky would just open in
not one person in the whole wide world
in the rain
my body when broken

its been a real privilege
you mean i wasnt there
the next one will take my seat
the second you walk into my bed
when the sky opened up a bit of snow
like a song on your mouth
you should be able to sing
when the heart stops beating
when the sky opens up
its never easy
the second that this is over
is never enough
the clouds are still
they seem to me this morning
like the skin
and my hands all blue
when everything changes its just that
if im gonna be up all night
its fine by me
its going down
you have a new skin
but the ocean in the room
doesnt go away
were having a celebration
my house is burning it was
is like nothing to do with my life
there will be time enough to lie about why
thats not a bird
when things get very dark
im going to tell you a secret?

the first thing this one sees?
a white picket fence
and then the other one sees a light
my heart is going like a drum
it wont stop playing
i dont think i know myself
in its own way
i was like
im in hell
the sun still shines
just when it gets dark at my house
the song the old man sings
but the world is ending
and someone wants something else
you know what this is
this is the feeling we have
when somethings not right with this
and it doesnt matter
ive been looking for
well go back to bed i guess
the way i see the stars above the bed
will keep us warm you think
well just sleep it off tonight
the first thing is that the sun
when nothing is not right with this
when things dont quite go
the next one cant wait
on better deals
for a moment like this
i just get this

its too late

were both going out tonight

my hand can barely

ill wait for you

after my head hits the pillow

because i dont think

i know that you dont

dont know why i know that

i dont know why i know

it might be that thing again

i was at a concert the night we were

when you were just leaving

there was somebody i wanted

something inside that i couldnt

that never should have been

left out

you just came home tonight

im getting more and more nervous

its time for another

i might do some harm with it

i think about the first

i wish that i wasnt this way

cause you have no choice

you have to learn whats true and whats wrong

you are like a child and a mother

there in your mothers house again

in some way

i need to go outside right now

and try this some more

i think about you

what you had on your mind
was always this far away
we should be able to do
whatever you want to do
you can make all the right decisions
about your own time
but i cant make it stop
that when the time comes
it will all be very clean
with no trace and nothing left
we might be all alone
when this is done
i hope you can understand
when i leave it all here with you
i am in love with all of this
the next thing this one looks at
is not this person at all
the heart stops beating
it will not be very nice of it
im never going to be with my friends
because one day they all will die
so do they matter to you
the last thing you see is
my heart stops beating
and i dont think that
there is anyway to live
the next one looks at the moon
you dont want to see what i see
in your eyes or your eyes
when the blood

is going out
of some of my best friends
when the ocean licks a beach
it never goes away
the waves go down in the tide
and the heart beats
when i was younger i didnt like the world
i only liked a lot of people
if you dont remember who
itll be all right with them
when they all came to their senses
when the time passes
and then you know
what to think about
when you think about whats true
and then i think about what you said
when we were having it
if you dont remember me at all
you know that the best thing i can do
is go on living
and i remember the way that it was
i got more than the last one
got it all so i just won
so i just cant wait
i should go now
when i was younger i liked a lot
of the wrong people
when you said something else
when the day is over and everything is said
my body will go away

and the next one cant wait
on a better deal
you are like a child
in your mothers house again
in some way
i know there must be a reason
that i cannot see it all the way down
the world is ending and
i wish i wasnt this way
because you have no choice
i love you too
and that this would disappear
my heart has just stopped

AND THE SOUND OF VOICES NEARBY

All I want
is to walk
in the palm-
lined hollow.
I no longer
sleep at night,
the problems
I could see
I cannot, and
that's all I have
to say. (There
is nothing
after this.)

WE'RE ONE SHOT WAITING FOR THE LIGHT/BATTLE IN THE SKIES

Barbed wire, in the drowsy surf,
makes a pattern like a mirror.
You can call me tomorrow
and I'll explain a light camera,
a code to be master,
a projector with my name on it,
and a sign of the grave.
So, will you come to my farewell
party? I'll come if you do.
I thought I heard myself fall
down the stairs a lot last night.

Collected Experimentalisms
2001-2004

Világos is an acute and brilliant poet, writing on being done wrong by the fiction of time and the system of the city. His is the poetry of the city that looks out into the night, time's winged sparrow, and notes the sky, knowing that there are few takers, but wanting the praise anyway. It is a manifesto for the protest poetry of the future, a classic in the tradition of Allen Ginsberg's Howl.
—Lizzie Violin, *Lost Form Murders*

Even in its war, or rather war of rhetoric and art, it creates room for the imagination, for the bodily act of constructing meaning. Világos has given us a collection of the temporal equivalent of large-scale physical protests, full of auspicia mundi and humus hile signs. 'We shall be citizens of the real, we shall not die in vain.' In the chaos of rebellion, new things will be born and the old, the patterned, will be left to die.
—Nicolette Grenadine, *Sunday*

This book is not only monumental, but also endlessly entertaining. It is organized by theme, and within each theme, not always by characters, but by subjects. The process of building these themes has been so complex and strange that it seems as though the true theme of the book is what Világos himself has called 'the graphic process'.
— Ricky Cole, *How to Die in Paris*

'For what is time, but the river in which everything that could not be has to flow through?' These are the most arresting lines in Világos' work. They are not just elegantly weird; they are a phenomenological ontology of the formative, disjunctive period of one's life. At the centre of the book is an interrogation of time in flux; of arrival and departure, reflection and dispersion, dreams and text, planning and co-creation. These are shifts in the distance between past, present and future. They are recognisable reflections of the changing geography of life. It is often said that literature is ultimately about a search for home. Világos is, perhaps, our most interesting and definitive answer to that search.
— Matthew Mitero, *City of Geist*

Világos takes us through the problem of reference and out the other side. In an age of ultra high definition televisions which seem more real than real, literature remains a powerful technology to awaken us out of our stupefactions and stupid actions. The work here both critiques and expands radical publishing praxis into dimensions of prolific labour within the anonymity of the imaginary domain (Drucilla Cornell). By dwelling in alternative references, the power to shoot objects in the volatile field of cultural production is stimulated via simulation and the synthetic. Much of the future has been done and our job as readers is to recover its latent energy in the Now.
— Ziddy Ibn Sharam, *Acharenement*

© 2022 U. G. Világos. All rights reserved; no part of this book may be reproduced by any means without the publisher's permission. Please purchase an original copy directly from U. G. Világos.

The author has asserted their right to be identified as the author of this Work in accordance with the Copyright, Designs and Patents Act 1988

EDITOR'S NOTE:
> The word 'gábor,' an Hungarian name, is the shortened form of the name Gabor. I use it in this publication because it seems to indicate that U. G. Világos' translation is the same as the 1997 Hungarian edition. The author states on his official website that his dates are sometimes different from the original, but I have been unable to find anything that confirms this in either the articles by James Nettles and Nina L. Shaw. Perhaps this is not something that has been widely discussed, however, so here we are.

FURTHER READING:
> Recommended by the editor of Solidarity Press, for the most comprehensive biography on the history of Világos's work, read *Villages Burning, The Work of U.G. Világos*.

If you are in the Central Greater University's General Studies program, there is a one credit short course entitled U. G. Világos. This course is described on the CGU website as follows:

> U. G. Világos is one of the most remarkable writers from Hungary. In 1967 Világos wrote a play, in which he sought to confront the historical tragedy of his time by entering the deepest depths of himself and presenting something novel: a sort of tragic self-criticism. His work, taking the form of fiction and non-fiction, and also long poems and short novels, reflects the epochal changes that took place in Hungarian literature, as well as in Europe at large.

Cover designed by Aaron Kent
Edited and typeset by Aaron Kent
Licensed for publication by Discovery Jones Library Ltd.
Translated from the Hungarian by U. G. Világos
Articles by James Nettles and Nina L. Shaw
Research into the meaning of the texts by David P. Miller
Written in English by U. G. Világos

CONTENTS

I.

You Killed My Cousin in a Drive-by	11
Brains 'n' Cake	12
Oh God I've Peaked!!!	14
Waiting for the Show to go on	16
Deranged Funny and Sad	17

II.

because money works in queues	18
I will not judge you when we sit [...]	19
Fantasy Baseball Waiver Wire	20
Float-in	22
The Red Child	27

III.

A Darned Good Time	28
Lowballgeddon	29
John Lamb	30
The Night Before	32
Young Knuckle	33
Sunny Domino	34
The Giant Mouth/The Typhoon	36

IV.

The Hypochondriac	38
Big Bear's Wartime Farm Heroes	39
The Flesh Eating Bionic Squirrel	41
Muffin McWorms	42
Honey Badger	43

Song of the Dawn	44
Song of the Morning	45
The Side of the Pool	46
Daily Fables	47
Big Joe & the Cave of Bones	49

V.

Johnny 5 Fingers	52
Superman's Blackout	54
The Magnetic Fields at Zero Gravity	55
Kaiju Nightmare	56

VII.

I Bebop	59
Scaramouch Kazoo	60
Captain Kitten	61

VIII.

It's Hard to be Happy as a Bohemian	63
The Rockons	65
The New Gambit / The Koalabat	70
The Lightning Klaxon Riding Shotgun	71
Old Row Redux	72
Well-Fermented Crust	74
Bobby Stubbs and the Long Horns	75

IX.

O Galileo Where Art Thou Satellites	76

X.

Three Eight Songs	77
Mr. Kite's Worsted	78
3 Seasons of The O. C.	80
Freddy vs Jason VII: Flower Drum Song	81
I.M. Jonathan Livingston Seagull	83

XI.

Jenő's Ghost, The Unfinished Sympathy	85

XII.

The Endless Exploding Lights	86
The Millionaire Fire Fight	87
Wolfpack Beats Per Minute	88
High Tech Madness	89
The Road To Wrestlemania	90
Angry Hipster on Acid	91
I Seldom Pray to Rabies	92
Naval	94

XIII.

Adventures of the Upside-Down Boys	96
Beethoven's Thirteen Hundredth	98
If You Think There is Too Much Scent	102
Take Out a Gun and Blow off your Foot	103
Secret texts of a Horror Story	104
There All Right	106
Strong and Tall and Missing	107
Out Back to Worth into the Mind	109
The Last Night was the Last Night [...]	111

XIV.

This One's Tiny Friend	113
Tried to Remember the Party	114
those who got mummified to be [...]	116
Like Red Screaming from Home	118
My Angry Days	119
Three Starving	120
Last Year is Swimming in a [...]	121

XV.

I'm Honestly Only Writing Because [...]	122
and the sound of voices nearby	128

Acknowledgements	131

Fell from the wagon / I guess / it's my own fault
—Band Ten, *Sickness*

You were destined for greatness
—The Melody Experience, *What Are You Waiting For?*

Why are you gonna do it? / When you know it's never gonna work? / Why do you think that you got to do it? / If I don't do it, will you come through?
—Down!, *Wolves*

The lower side of the ground / can't you see / I'm okay in my own mind
—Planet More, *Ironic*

I tried to tell myself that it was a good life but now it's too late / That's all I have to say / I'm sorry, but I'm running out of time
—The Glorious Sundays, *New Town*

Possession / (That ghost is) mine, mine, mine
—Yoghco, *Young and Daring*

My right leg shook and my lips parted / I looked around my head / I didn't know where I was
—Cupid Con, *You're Not Alone*

We decided to take the long way back / built a home
—James Chase, *Such Thing As A Dragon*

Mondays you only want to sleep / get out of bed, be present
—The Glory Years, *The Things We Do For Love*

I'm not the same as I used to be / I'm just a passing, mortal shell
—Dead Sheppard, *Cry For You*

Now here I am, there is nothing left / I will keep telling the truth / I don't give a damn / I'll cry all night
—Ash Head, *Gutted*

Do I have to be that type of man / I'm so confused...
—West Rhythm, *Siding Up*

It's so easy to let my mind get the best of me / Easy to believe I'm a mess and no one understands / But, for now, I'll just be *Dollar* sick
—Moreso Than, *The Pretty Game*

If you ask me / I can't even decide / No one really knows me / Then what do I know? / It's so easy to say / The only thing to do / Is keep searching
—Selina Sirens, *All Of You*

But why can't I look in the mirror / No one understands / I'm just a nobody...
—The Mourning, *Some Name To Shame*

I've got a messed up family / Yeah, I'm broke / It's nice being free, I'm free
—The Rink, *Moth Mouth*

Who told you to turn on your side / Are you sick? / I'm just a little tired / But why am I so tired? / I'm just a normal guy
—Freehouse, *Into The Wheel*

My mind's wonky / These walls ain't enough / And he's outside, falling apart
Hun Garland, *I And Herring Over*

For Anne,
who built me a house and made it a home

For Scout,
Who came when the angels were knocking

For Fox,
Who I wish will never speak a word

For Mum & Dad,
Who loved defiant of my wasting away

For Richard,
Who wanted to know if I was alive

For Aunt Kay,
Whose voice was so loud it made all other voices louder

For Nan,
Who always cheered us up when we were down

For Uncle Wally,
Whose will to live was strong

For all the wayward souls
Who cross our paths

For Norbert,
Whose tender love knows no bounds

For Aunt Mary,
Whose forgiveness gave me room to do the same

For Joe & Cheryl,
Who've brought new light and new hope into our family

For Uncle Bub,
Whose curiosity never ceased

For Uncle Ralph,
Who taught me there's a lot of love in the world

For my brother,
Whose heart broke a thousand times

For Becky,
Whose smile brightens our every day

For Uncle Paul,
Whose arms are always open

For Michelle,
Whose love for music has forever changed my life

For Mark & Carly,
Whose kindness can't be measured

For Steph & Kevin,
Whose love knows no love

For my cousin,
Whose laugh makes our whole family laugh

For Myself,
Whose great potential will always fall short

BIBLIOGRAPHY

Shadows of Burgundy (Penny Dender, 1965)

The Lark Sings Wind (Jenoimissyou Books, 1965)

She'll Have Her Way (Sylvia's Sweet Shop, 1966)

Blood Orchid (Dennie Swann, 1966)

Esther Perel, Listen To Your Heart (The Cypher Press, 1966)

Ripe (Danube Down Publications, 1967)

A Shakespeare Rítus (Hamisított Shakespeare-szövegek, 1967)

Library Lion Inside Out (Hyperion, 1967)

Diane Speaks of Derrida, The Human Abstract (Kaleidoscope, 1967)

The Fashion Dog (Literally Arts, 1968)

Seven Days in the Lark's November (Jane Cooper Editions, 1968)

Panorama Reiki (Danube Down Publications, 1969)

Appropriation des Idoles Résistantes (Charrue Presse, 1969)

Xenophobia Olympics Games (Szívesen Látott Bevándorlók, 1969)

Az Ellenálló Bálványok Kisajátítása	(szántóprés, 1970)
Appropriation of the Resistant Idols	(Plough Press, 1970)
To This: Reportage On Revolutions, etc.	(A Touchstone Book, 1970)
Quilt	(Drum and book Club, 1971)
Think, Revolutions Everywhere	(Bell-nap Press, 1971)
Filling the Walls on Crinkleswell Road	(Humid Press, 1971)
North of Aries, South of Me	(Esplanade Books, 1972)
Radio Silence	(Kapcsolja be és ki újra, 1972)
A World in the Ocean, the Tower in Flames	(Stinging Nettle, 1972)
Centre of the Universe, the Mind in a Machine	(Hyper Atom, 1972)
Dialogue With a Visible Future	(Honesty Pubs, 1973)
Oraschin Tempa	(Daphniceleste, 1973)
Az Utcák Varázslók Nélkül	(Első szakasz Könyvek, 1973)
The Streets Without Magicians	(Knebel Verlag, 1973)
That Lark of Yours	(Collect Book, 1974)

Studies in the Vocabulary of Music	(Hyper Atom, 1974)
Words in Ink	(New Traditions, 1975)
Emerge	(International Tower of Poetry, 1975)
A Writ for the City	(Harmondsworth, 1976)
Time by This Time Tomorrow	(Bell-nap Press, 1976)
Thought Forms & Mistakes	(Intuit, 1977)
In Between Unbeing and Being	(Mary Lyons Publications, 1977)
Death Before Running	(A Slow Year, 1978)
You Used to Seem Lost To Us...	(Co-exit, 1979)
Poems, Material, & Other Notes on Ritual	(Jane Cooper Editions, 1979)
Vegetarianizmus	(A Stage Name, 1980)
A Plague of Doves	(A Postal Operation, 1980)
Sutras, Dawn's Head with Revelation	(Up-Holds, 1980)
On the Disappearance of Death	(All-A-Point, 1980)
Shod Maiden, Other Scenes	(First/Periodic Modern, 1981)

Magical Voices for Cthulhu	(Resplendent Voices, 1981
Of This Death I Pray Not and Father	(The Cypher Press, 1981)
Peculiar Souls	(Mid City Poetry Series, 1981)
Loose Leaf Tea Junction	(Belle-Beau Publishing, 1982)
Wearing a Skin of Visions	(Magic Republic, 1982)
Green Lights In Fence Woods & Falling Birds	(Humid Press, 1983)
Personalities Flocking	(First/Periodic Modern, 1983)
The Carcass of Vaudeville	(Jenoimissyou Books, 1984)
Terror of an American Tenor	(On-Yeh-Tod publishing, 1984)
Out of the Cold at Midnight	(Helicopter Gallery, 1984)
Being Happy as an Autodidact	(Repress Repeat Press, 1985)
A Shielded Coast Threatening To Blow	(A Swim Among the City, 1986)
Birds of the Breadfruit	(Send With Sender Press, 1986)
Tree-Empowered Memories of a Childhood	(Guilt of the Shell, 1986)
Water Will Never Cry Me To Sea	(Intodarkness, 1987)

A Shoreward Land and The Iron Raven	(Hyper Atom, 1987)
Waterwise	(Gotten Up and Left, 1987)
Ten Stages of Departure	(Dimmer Switch, 1987)
Hammered Screen	(Mid City Poetry Series, 1987)
Asledge	(An New-ish Thread Press, 1987)
Environmental Drama	(Xephaniwt Books, 1988)
Roses Were Fatalists	(Mumma-kin Press, 1988)
Public Aftershave and Piercings	(Lost The insulation, 1988)
A House of My Own	(Dressing Gown/Down, 1989)
Loyal to My own Decline	(I Came Here Looking For A Fight, 1989)
The Little Blue Book	(Red Deer Press, 1990)
The Last Thing I Remembered	(Splendid Buttons, 1990)
The Saffron Road	(Red-deer Press, 1990)
The Little Blue Book 2	(Red-deer Press, 1991)
Foster Girl	(Thinking Pixels Press, 1992)

The Thought Book	(Splendid Buttons, 1992)
One Long Day, with Optional Returns	(Reticulated Chipmunk, 1992)
The Little Blue Book 3	(Red-deer Press, 1992)
Woman is to man a cannon	(Thinking Pixels Press, 1992)
Easter Eggs for the Working Class	(Thinking Pixels Press, 1993)
Riding the Sunny Streak	(Splendid Buttons, 1993)
Don't Feed Him a Decadent Week	(Handtroll Publications, 1993)
Dream Wedding: An Afterword	(Finish the Soup Books, 1993)
Death in Summer, the Sequel	(Kovács Nagy Editions, 1993)
Talk of New York, Whispers of Dying Friends	(One K Cash Books, 1994)
Fekete Gömb: Világok 100,000	(Kovács Nagy Editions, 1994)
Black Sphere: 100,000 Worlds	(Loafing Cat, 1994)
A Chance You've Never Asked For	(Thinking Pixels Press, 1994)
Heat and Light	(Cracked Frame, 1994)
Black Dog-leaves, the Second Time Around	(The Blue Wheel, 1995)

Please We Would Like More Fruit (Underdream, 1995)

The Twin Restaurant (Pyramid Games, 1995)

Porcelán egy kitömött tehénből (Rajna-vidék, 1995)

Porcelain from a stuffed cow (Rhineland Press, 1995)

One Long Day, with an Optional Return (Reticulated Chipmunk, 1996)

From Other Worlds (Reticulated Chipmunk, 1996)

Vision Quest (Hi-Heena Books, 1997)

Marking Time (Cracked Frame, 1997

Cross in the Back (Archipelago Nation, 1997)

Caffeine Dreams (Whole Fox Books, 1998)

There is No Ever So Green Borne Deep (Hi-Heena Books, 1998)

Hurry Lying on the Deepening Grass (the Blue Wheel, 1998)

Would you do the Waiting (I Came Here Looking For A fight, 1999)

Striped People (Images in the Kitchen) (Jupiter Fruit Books, 1999)

On the Sheffield Express (Over The Phone Press, 2000)

The Language Of Ants	(Darkness At Midday, 2000)
This Feathered Land	(Darkness at Midday 2001)
Alien In Istanbul	(Seagreen Press, 2001)
Wanderweird in San Francisco	(Archipelago Nation, 2002)
All Fish Lie	(Conviction Affliction, 2002)
Songs of Ancient	(Hark Shadow, 2003)
Our New World	(Hark Shadow, 2003)
The Venus Syndrome	(Lined Out Marker, 2004)
The Other Line	(Shelter Skelter, 2004)
Put to Sleep	(Ord to an Echo, 2005)
Laced Notes	(Icycle Bicycle Press, 2005)
Year of your Visitation	(Punk House of Punk, 2006)
A Human Melancholy	(Temple Tether, 2007)
Empty Snow	(Literal Translations, 2008)
Bewitching Turn	(Punk House of Punk, 2008)

The Leaving Song	(SoapBox, 2009)
Steal Please	(Hundred Tundra, 2009)
It took ten hundred lonely words	(Pastel Pastel Pastel, 2010)
From your end	(Flame Witch, 2011)
Post-Capitalist Minds	(Constitutional Letters, 2011)
Speak of Beauty	(Art & Brains, 2012)
The Atomic Fashion Book	(Nebula Nebula, 2012)
Nothing and Nobody	(Hyper Gravity, 2013)
Above and Under	(Literary Workshop, 2013)
Mothership Suite	(Purple, 2014)
To Live	(Stride on Books, 2015)
The Wreathed Caves	(Earth Editorial, 2015)
The Giant House	(Kaiju Skull, 2016)
Older Colder Blues	(Baseball Bunt Books, 2016)
I'll Tell You Why I Had a Mother	(Winter, 2017)

The Day Of My First Birth	(Asterley, 2018)
The Moon and Salt	(Asterley, 2018)
My Blue Nightgown	(The Pinch, 2019)
The Night Before The Day (For A Bear)	(The Resident Review, 2019)
A Short Tale From the Big Guy Upstairs	(Intriguing Deaths Press, 2019)
Eating Salt: On Memory & Food	(The Pinch, 2020)
A Place for Flowers: A Family Memoir	(Intriguing Deaths Press, 2020)
Trouble Sleeping: A Memoir in a Single Sentence	(Weeping, 2021)
Nocturnes	(Tiny Lights, 2022)
The Blue in the East	(University of Ogacihc Press, 2022)
The Little Blue Book	(Red-deer Reprise, 2022)
Myrtle, Violet, and Me	(Rent Free, 2023)
Sketches In The Air	(Broken Sleep Books, 2023)
Blue-Cello	(Jellyfish, 2023)
For All The White City	(Plucky Little Rat Press, 2024)

Literal Love Poems   (Ezcsakegyunalmasszerelmesverseskötet, 2024)

All The Days: A Memorial for U. G. Világos   (Coffee Anonymous, 2025)

POSTHUMOUS BOOKS

The Little Red Book: A Remembrance (Sleeping & Weeping, 2028)

The Little White Book (Broken Sleep Books, 2028)

The Big Yellow Book (Coffee Anonymous Press, 2028)

The Long-awaited Blue Book (Rent Free, 2028)

Wake, or An Abridgement (Jellyfish, 2028)

Touches, in The Blue in the East (Dedalus, 2028)

I, Architect: A Memoir of Memory & Survival (Coffee Anonymous, 2028)

Eggs on the Stairs (Coffee Anonymous, 2029)

The Story of His Hands (Charnwood Court, 2029)

U.G.'s House (The Last Place, 2029)

A Long Summer Dead (Visual Confirmation, 2030)

PRAISE FOR VILÁGOS

The Lark Sings Wind is a wonderful contribution to the literary landscape, nothing less than extraordinary, incredibly lyrical poetry that demands attention only to go on increasing in its tenderness, its cleverness, its interest and its deepness.
—N. O. Lannorth, *The Daily Telegram*

Writing as poetry that is novel in verse
 —Anna Grave-Simmons, *Sunday Mag*

The Fashion Dog is a book that broods... rich in wit, in complex and interesting imagery... rarely less than deeply moving, but rarely more than superficially interesting.
 —Hamish McCay, *Contemporary Review*

The Fashion Dog is the worst book I've ever read. It's so boring that if it were an animal I'd put it out of its misery. It's also so badly written I think you should just burn it.
 —Jen Wills, *Slalom*

Artful, impressive, pungent... Világos is one of the most original voices in a lifetime.
 —Donald Leavitt, *The New York Book Preview*

Exhilarating poetry that moves the mind with virtuosity and the heart with power and tenderness.
 —Barb Spitz, *The York Ghost Magazine*

A powerful and beautiful portrayal of the disintegration of marriage, by a remarkable writer, buy *Quilt* today.
—Sandra Chorter, *Trampolinemagazine*

Terribly boring work that pivots between experimental and detrimental. I wouldn't recommend this to the neighbour's dog.
—Morty Lanyard, *NEVER NOT DULL*

Stunningly evocative... both lyrical and passionate... with a tender sense of longing, and a distinctive voice for each poem. In Világos' hands, the poetic line is not an end in itself, but something fundamental to reading.
—Alice Thompson, *The Irish Indie*

An astonishingly inventive writer... a poet who takes his readers on a long journey through complicated and treacherous questions of responsibility and of love.
—Pamela Carter, *The Indie Audit*

Beautiful and moving... rare in its power.
—Jan Morris, The Independent

Wonderful, brave, funny, sad, exuberant and inventive... a beautiful collection... Világos writes with passion and feeling.
—Richard Washington, *The Harrington Post*

There are stories of all kinds here... [and] there is a shrewd understanding of what it means to be a human being in a changing world, but that's all he can offer in what is a woeful offering.
—Harry Boston, The Borden Globe

A nightingale of poetry... astonishing... [and] stunning.
—Anthony Jonas, *The Poetic Encroachment*

A revelation... brilliant.
—Justine Heap, *Justified Euphoria*

Poetry like a modern's dream... a gift from the land... the finest, most ambitious poetry since the playwright R. B. Avon... a celebration... delicate and piercing... in beautiful verse.
—C. R. Delmar, *The Book Review*

It's the most intelligent, the most satisfying, and the most important, of his three collections... the perfect way to end the *Lark* trilogy.
—T. H. Elorb, *Flaming Carrot*

The most penetrating, the most successful, and the most mature of all his collections.
—Harry Engel, The Borden Globe

Hauntingly beautiful. A striking voice... his tone, his almost lyrical imagery, his beauty of sound, his compassionate humanism and his joy in every day make this collection a singular treasure.
—J. J. Powers, *The Independent Journal of Poetic Space*

A sustained tour de force in poetic form... [I]f anyone is going to repeat Perec's feat, it is he.
—John Jeremiah J. Sullivan, *The Literary Review*

A poet with a vision... poetry of many colours... transgressive and vulnerable and yet commanding.
—C. R. Smiley, *Justified Euphoria*

Világos, so long a thorn in the side of censorship and the literary establishment, continues his great escape through a borderless poetic wilderness.
—Eleanor Freeman, *The Gin & Tonic*

A book that dazzles... tremendous language... poetry that can be read as prose... but shouldn't be.
—Brandy M. Burton, *The Parisian Review*

A searing exploration of inner lives... an urgent and inimitable text... Pungent, enthralling and astonishing.
—T. F. S. Telegraph, *Frosted Tips*

Pure shit, wretched writing from a wretched writer.
—Robert Loyal, *Stripes*

A startling, passionate, funny, heart-breaking work... liturgical and brilliantly powerful... by a writer at the height of his powers, Világos deserves a wide audience.
—L. F. Dion, *The Telegram*

Grief and love are so fascinating that they can raise even the most self-centred writer to new heights.
—Emma E. Hirsch, *The Sunday Morning Herald*

A majestic, exhilarating book filled with poetry, wit, prose and art... [and] a testimony to Világos's gift for evoking and making human a wide range of experiences... [a] noble and courageous work.
—Jean-Louis Monet, *Le Monet*

I read this and regretted reading it. I hate to say that. The idea is wonderful, but this is a big work about a big family, and in that big work, the family is not so great.
—I. M. C. Ewan, *Sunday*

His work is bold, intimate, demanding, and challenging... emotionally powerful and enrapturing.
—G. Lombardo, *The Hundreds & Thousands*

I've always felt Világos is a terrible writer, that his work is just a bad act. [but] 'Nocturnes' is a performance, it's his memoir of his insomnia's occupation of his grief. If ever a work took me on a ride into its own dream, it's Világos's book.
—Liam H. Richards, *The Fourth Moon*

Like many great poets, Világos excels in arresting images, haunting stories and extended metaphors... 'Nocturnes' is a devastating book, and the ending could serve as the punch line to a really tragic joke.
—Miles McCharrey, *Flaming Carrot*

A writer of wonderful lyric powers, Világos is equally at home in the idioms of formal poetry and in the jargon of a fine political poem... 'Nocturnes' is bold, fearless, and emotional, and it's a good thing it was.
—J. U. P. Dice, *The Dreams*

Világos's poetry is god-awful. I hate him, I hate his work, and I hate being forced to live in the same world as him.
—Steven Adamsbergh, *Poetic Lyricism Journal*

ENDNOTES

1. The same inversion of the political order occurs in Beding's *The Turn*, trans. Alberto Todansc (Cambridge: Polity Bureau, 2007), pp. 21–22. In *The Turn*, we also encounter a striking citation of the last of Beding's early texts, 'On the Concept of Class':

> Insofar as the concept of 'class' designates a particular form of the structure of political-administrative power, the 'transcendental formula' refers to the condition of possibility of any form of political administration and all legislative measures" (p. 32).

One may observe that the passage cited is about a transcendental formula that transcends the concept of class, whereas, in *The Turn*, the passage cited is about a transcendental formula that designates a condition of possibility of class struggle. In that sense, the passage cited in *The Turn* has the effect of bringing back into the world the world of the concept.

2. For an account of the way the concept of class is transformed in a text that presents itself as a critical-materialist philosophy of class, see the first two chapters of Gerrard Calvinio, *Le classique: La philosophie et la classe travailleuse* (Paris: Éditions la Brel Mer, 1999).

3. The word here translated as "rule" is elquḍā'. I have translated it as "law" to emphasize its legal connotation. The term was used in legal discussions to describe the relation of a legal rule to its sources and the relation of a legal rule to its purpose. It also connotes an authority that is above or that gives rules to people. In these respects, it is similar to the French term loi, although loi designates also an order of things that precedes the authority of the law, a conception that has been developed in recent thinking about law. In these ways, the two terms are similar, although it is the jurists who have developed the legal meaning of the term and its extension to the realm of government.

4. For a more complete account of this controversy, see Madrigal S. Madrigal, *Reading The Origins of Concept: Lokan's Dialogue of the Dead* (London and New York: Continuous Concern, 2005), 71-96; and Géza Marx, *The Young Lokan: The Genesis of his Early Political Philosophy* (Boston: Klaw Claw Academic Publishers, 2001), 55-59.

5. See Lokan, 'The Modern Ideology of the City: Reflections on the Capitalist Urban Experience' in *Lokan and the Political: A New View of History, Thought and Society*, edited by Madrigal S. Madrigal (London and New York: Continuity Credits, 2005), p. 103.

[MISSING ENDNOTES]

11. The terms here translated as "system" and "complex" are lāṭhīn and maktabīn. Both terms have been translated as "system" in earlier work, but it has now been established that neither is equivalent with the term muktaṛṣṭra which refers to a system of social production, exchange and distribution. 'System' and 'complex' are both more general terms than 'social production'. This becomes evident when the various subsystems (i.e., economic and legal, political, educational and ideological) are compared, which is what Lokan did in his early works, *especially History and Class Consciousness* (Lokan 1978: vol. 1, ch. 3). His later works, especially on Hegel and on political economy, deal more extensively with social production and social change in general. (See his 'Karl Marx: An Introduction to His Critique of Political Economy,' in The *Young Lokan*, edited by Ruth Dre (London: Journal Time, 2004), chs. 3-9.)

12. This line is not found in G. Lokan, *Historical Materialism* (Lokan 1978: vol. 2, ch. 10).

13. As far as the phrase 'a political economy of the consciousness' is concerned, this can refer to only one of the early Lokan books (see the discussion above), *History and Class Consciousness*.

14. The original says, '… the class struggle as a specific historical process;' it should be '… as an objective historical process, the class struggle.'

15. In the original, 'a revolutionary,' instead of 'irrevocably… as such.'

16. He actually wrote 'a dialectical system… with its own law of development…' The term 'law of development' would not be fully expressed in Hungarian until the 1930s. In his later writings, Lokan elaborated the concept and wrote that the dialectical method as a method of scientific understanding becomes a method of scientific thinking; it is not just a mere methodological means to be employed after the fact.

ACKNOWLEDGEMENTS

My thanks to the editors of these journals and anthologies where some of these poems or versions of them have been published:

Cave Spring Poems, Voices From A Quiet Lake, Life in Flatbush, Long Landings, Boomerang, Selected Ruminations, Cheat-Sheet Ballads, The Tease and the Punch, The Borderlands of Euphoria, Illuminations: Poems by Men in Their Twenties, Shakespeare's Purgatory, East of Kant, Chronicle of an Undone, Hanging Loose: A Revolution in Stages, Yellow Flash: A Poet Speaks, Don Quixote's Dog, The Village of Concrete Poetry, What Becomes of our Dead God?, The Rivers and Tides of Kukiyo Hayashi, Justified Euphoria, Ó, God-nest: Carts and Chronicles of Nowhere, Carousel of Devotion, Home and Longing, In A Sea of Nature, Preliminary Papers on Aleister Crowley, Classically Martial, Crack Open The Coffin, The Up-And-Coming Poets, Bats, Bi-Centennial Trilogy, Memoranda de Oxi, Sonic Innovation, A Day for White Elephants, Flash Grant and the Jacuzzi Race, The Vortex: Poems of New Zealand, Pastiche, Chants for the Dead, Ampersand Anthology, The Lunar Year, Retiring Orpheus, Formica, A Short History of Sonnet 10, Visible Frictions, Reuben, Weep, Reading in a Wig, The Night Circus, In the Valley of the Elephants: Conversations with the Poets of Budapest, Visible Frictions, The Hunger, Will to Live, A Light That Never Dies, The Separate Church, We, The Little Tree, Night Song, Regarding the Pain of Others: A Book of Absolution, A Good Poem for Today, A Book of Negative Daydreams, Mistaken Attraction, Moxy, Rhinoceros, A Perfect Mourning for the Streets, Dysfunction 2.0, O.D.'s: On Evolution and Revisionism,

The Poetry of the Future, Total Poetry, Geriatric Poets: In All Their Primitive Glory, Melancholy, Blue Language, Atrocities, Garbage Palace, Flaming Carrot, Yellow Jacket, Robot Utopia, Whole Cycle, Alphabet Sketchbook: New Bop! New Wave!, and *Life as a Slow Motion Trainwreck.*

Many thanks to Jammm Golden, editor of My *Name Is Come So Far,* and a winner of the Izzy Fishingwood Foundation Award for Excellence in Literature, for her permission to use her photo of Shelly Murphy's house in the Bronx.

BIOGRAPHY

U. G. Világos is a poet, editor and teacher. His new collection, *The Mostly Fictitious Man*, is forthcoming in Summer 2023, and a collection of flash-poems titled *Troubles, Nights, Meditations & Memoranda for a Passing Smile* is forthcoming in 2024. He is the editor of *We Still Use Poetry: The 2nd Quarterly Anthology of Contemporary Poetry in the Margins*. He sometimes writes as Discovery Jones. As Jones he has published the poetry chapbook *How to Survive a Shark Attack* and the novels *Possession, 1972* and *The Last Tracer*.

Collected Experimentalisms
2005-2008

SPRING

In the vast nothingness of night

I am reminded of
how infinitesimally
small
the nature of grief is

If I push my eyes at a certain angle I can see   two   moons moving away from us/you. Everything has moved from you.

As we hurl

through space,

we clutch our knees

and imagine ourselves

as sentient balls of yarn

buoyed by their own

scientific progress.

The window superimposes me as larger than trees.

I don't like that.

Nobody deserves that.

I've been trying to write the silence of your death.

I want to write the silence of your death.

Your death, so silent.

My grief, so small, so loud.

Every house is a light switch away from a home.

I've been plugging
cords into mushrooms
trying to
trying
trying
trying to
convert bio-energy
of fungi
&
decomposition
into music
you could hear
somewhere in
the vast nothingness of night.

A will only matters if you're alive to see it actioned.

SUMMER

The whirr of carrion into flesh,

the flash of red,

the mole's last act to be redug.

Bat loops * Tkk Tkk bird roosts * Late lethargic butterfly *
Lawnmower bee graveyard shift

Paraphernalia of frog-spawn shifts

Loose, limp wind solitary

The cows bed down

Cautious cavitation

Doppler fly flies

The banded thief is alone, yelling.

Ultrasound finds the sky's heartbeat as a purr.

Does the earth hum in feline?

Poe's bird shouts once and then

                              A recursive cry—hedge to hedge

A return in a different pitch.

        These things carry on without you.

        Why do you not return in a different pitch?

Things you could return as:

3000 tiny gnats waiting to be swallowed
A bat, denied of flight, throwing itself from the second floor
Flying ants stripping their anniversary wings
A nest chewed through from underneath
The Tkk Tkk bird, silent for wind-chimes
Steel shrinking with a click
A retained bee's single house
A windmill clicking
Poe's birds vocal tennis
A raised wolf announcing itself
Bonfire fresh in midnight air
The stream and the Tkk Tkk bird in harmony

Things you do return as:

Muzzled static
Grief spread across sleep
Tsunami winds
Dreams to ghost and haunt

Nothing. Nothing at all.

AUTUMN

A light flicks off,

                                                    somewhere

a woodpecker

Is wrapping its tongue

around its skull

                I am wrapping my tongue

                    around my skull

                I am pressing my teeth

                    into my neck

A noise, like a predator's battery, discharges.

Like the memory of you discharging itself.

The heat bites, licks the corners of the sky

My knee pops out I am weakened

A painted red opens its translucent leaves and flies home.

The vampire bird salutes,
returns with another,
returns with another.

Poe's birds harmonise,
a chorus of knocks.

A noise like a gong
anticipating its own impact

Somebody is approaching—a quad bike.

The pram is still out and I have been asked three times.

The cows are blood-curdled.

I will later learn you never called out.

You.

Alone on the floor.

Alone under the table.

Too proud to cry.

Too far from the Danube to swim home.

Don't forget the eggs

the banded thieves will eat them.

Cows scream / they scream in transport / they scream in knowing

Rain like a round of applause / Shadow of an angel / watching the gutters

                                                                                                         drip

WINTER

When you died,
I was promised silence
but I can still hear it all
I can still hear everything
you have contorted to miss.

This grief carries in both sound

in sound

and space

in space

We are back to

silent stream
lights fading
clicking on
f a d i n g
clicking on
m o t i o n

We never spoke about
The bramble's pinch
The translucency of stillness
The sky painted blush
So why would we start now?
Why am I here, approaching nature
for answers from a condition
we never cared to configure.

Finally
an ultrasound
a rumble East to West
tracing the long lost sun
& its immense gravitational pull

YEAR AFTER YEAR ONWARDS
Epilogue

We make our way to morning,
in the corner of the field a nest,
an egg in its throat,
the TKK TKK bird's gallbladder intact.

An Eastern Imperial flies at tree level
as we walk up and down,
a hole in a carrier bag,
your ashes everywhere but here.

This early light is still
bright orange as in a painting
from a time before time,
not forgotten but a mystery

We are in the mud and stones
of the river as somewhere
the day and the dark
meld into one another like time

And then I am in the nest.
The stream is a river,
the mud looks like an ocean.
You are on the banks.

You are in the river, crowing,
heading out to sea once more.
You are reborn, boundless,
a jellyfish again and again.

You are on the river,
with your mother and grandmother
and the water that never stops
to be held with these hands.

The sky and the sea,
the stones and the stars
And you, everywhere,
a crow in a nest catching worms.

It is too difficult to hold this world
in the palms of our hands.
Can we live together today
and die together once more?

Collected Experimentalisms
2009-2012

HERE WHAT LICKS SINS

I'm sorry we're moving, I'm sorry we're moving again. Our last stop will be your hometown. The one with all of the hauntings. This is how the world ends. A ghost is never what you think, you can't catch a ghost like you catch a butterfly. A storm of empty crows perches on the telephone lines in August, and someone you know will die and they'll die by a bullet, a knife, an explosion or a long string of cigarettes. They'll die of a bad dream of a long winter. They'll die by their own hand. The way I die is by breaking my back while trying to make a window where there isn't one. It looked easy and took less than a minute. We don't talk about these things, the ways we can make it all go away. You can't kill a ghost, but if you could wouldn't you be tempted to try? There's too much noise, too much static in my head. When we're done, we'll sit out the silence in the woods with you. We'll be quiet and patient with ourselves as we watch this world burn.

THE WINE OF SIN IS HERE

Sorry, we're moving, sorry, we're moving again. Our last stop is a town like yours. The only people who dream about how the world will end are never who you think. You can't dream like a butterfly. In August, void clouds will buzz over the phone lines and someone you know will be shot, stabbed, blown up or killed by a long chain of cigarettes. They die from bad sleep & long winters. They die by their own hands, to break my back and create a window where there is none. It's easy and takes less than a minute. We are not talking about them, but about ways to remove them. You can't kill a ghost, but if you could, wouldn't you be tempted to try? I have a lot of noise in my head all the time. When we are done, we will sit quietly with you in the forest. While this world burns we will remain calm and patient.

HERE IS THE WINE OF SIN

Sorry, I'm moving, sorry, I'm moving again. Our final destination is a town like yours. You would think that people are the only ones who dream about the end of the world, but animals do too. You can't dream like a butterfly. In August, a blank cloud will appear over the phone line and someone you know will be shot, stabbed, blown up, and killed with a cigarette. They'll die from lack of sleep or a long winter. They will die from cutting back and creating a windowless space. It's not about them, it's about ways to get rid of them. You can't kill a ghost, but if you could, would you try? I have a constant noise in my head. When we are done, we will sit with you quietly in the forest. Let's be patient and calm while this all burns.

IT IS THE WINE OF SIN

Sorry I'm gone, sorry I'm gone again. Our ultimate goal is to showcase your city. You will never believe that only people dream of the end of the world. You can't dream like a child. A blank cloud will appear over the telephone line in August and someone you know will be smoked, stabbed, blown up, and killed. They'll die from a prolonged exposure to cold, by their own hands. Go create a windowless room, it's easy and takes less than a minute. You can't kill a ghost, but if you could, would you try? A funny voice is playing in my head. Finally, we will live peacefully with you in the forest. Let us be patient and calm while this world is burning.

WINE AND PLUM EVIL

Sorry for passing by, sorry for leaving again. Our main goal is to put your city in the sunlight. Never believe that only humans want the world to end. I can't dream like a child. In August, an empty cloud appears on the phone, and someone you know smokes, cuts, explodes, and kills. They die from prolonged exposure to cold. Create a windowless room. It's not about them, it's about getting rid of them. You can't kill Satan, but if you could, would you try? I hear funny voices in my head. Indeed, we live with you in peace in the forest. Let's live patiently and calmly while the world burns.

BAD WINE AND ONIONS

I'm sorry I got lost, I'm sorry I got lost again. Our main goal is to experience our city. Don't think that people don't want the world to end. I can't dream like a child. In August, the phone will be empty and someone you know will smoke, get hurt, explode, and get killed. They'll die in your arms while you create a mirror-free room. You can't kill the devil, but what if you could try? I hear strange voices in my head. Yes, we will live with you in peace in the forest. Be patient, the world is burning.

BED WIRE

Sorry I got lost again. Our main goal is to get to know the city. Don't think that people don't want this world to end. I do not dream like a child. In August, your phone is empty and someone you know smokes, gets hurt, flies, falls, dies. Cut a room without glass. You can't kill demons, but what happens when you try? I heard strange voices in my head. Yes, we live in peace with you in the forest. Be patient, the world is burning.

HIS BED

Sorry, I got lost again. Our main goal is to know the city. Don't think that people don't want the world to end. I don't have dreams like a child. Your phone will be empty in August and people you know who suffer from smoke inhalation will die. Cut to an empty room. You can't kill the monster, so what happens when you try to kill a monster? I hear a strange voice in my head. Yes, we are in the forest. Be patient.

BED

Sorry, I got lost again, our main goal was to get to know the city. Don't think people don't want the world to end. I had no dreams when I was young. Your phone will be free in August. Someone you know has also been suffocated or killed by smoke. Cut to an empty grave. You can't kill the devil or the strange voice in my head. We are in the forest. Breathe first. Breathe.

BLED

Unfortunately, I still haven't found it. Our priority is to explore the city. Don't think that people don't like the end of time. I never dreamed when I was young. Someone you know has died from smoking. Cut to an empty tomb. You can't kill the devil or the supernatural in my head. We are in the forest. First, breathing.

MAYBE NOT

Unfortunately, I didn't see it, the main thing is to see the city. Don't think people don't like Day of the Dead. I never saw that as a kid. I know people who have died from smoking. Arrests were made. You can't kill the ghost of my boss. The stranger took his first breath and cried.

PROBABLY NOT

Unfortunately, I haven't seen it in the city yet. I don't think people like Day of the Dead. I never faced anything like this when I was young. I know that tobacco is dead. He was arrested. You cannot kill a soul. The first man was confused and cried.

I'M SAD

I go to town often. I am not happy today. I don't know him since childhood. We know he smokes. You can catch me and destroy the monster. I cried at first

RELEASE

I often go to the city. I don't like that. We know they suck. You can destroy monsters. I cried at first.

FUSES

I live in a big city. I don't know if you like it or not but we know it's important. cry and die.

CRY

I live in a big city. I know pain.

GLOSSARY OF POEMS

#

3 Seasons of The O. C.	204

A

Acknowledgements	299
A Darned Good Time	151
Adventures of the Upside-Down Boys	224
and the sound of voices nearby	262
Angry Hipster on Acid	216
Ardent	22

B

Bad Wine and Onions	360
because money works in queues	246
Bed	363
Bed Wire	361
Beethoven's Thirteen Hundredth	226
Bibliography	278
Big Bear's Wartime Farm Heroes	162
Big Joe & the Cave of Bones	172
Biography	301
Bled	364
Bobby Stubbs and the Long Horns	199
Brains 'n' Cake	217
BURNYOURCATHEDRALSTOTHEGROUND	21

C

Captain Kitten	184
CAVITATION	20
Circles	14
Contents	270
Cronus (Home of the Soldiers)	180

D

Daily Fables	170
Delfin	19
Deranged Funny and Sad	244
Destruction on Film	400

E

Endnotes	296

F

Fantasy Baseball Waiver Wire	143
Float-in	145
Foreword	7
Freddy vs Jason VII: Flower Drum Song	205
fuses	369

H

Here is the Wine of Sin	357
Here What Licks Sins	355
High Tech Madness	213
His Bed	362

Honey Badger	166
Honeyed Songs	16
hope is a dangerous way to maim yourself	23

I

I Bebop	182
I saw the world as a "Big Show."	
If You Think There is Too Much Scent	230
I'm Honestly Only Writing Because I'm Scared [...]	255
I.M. Jonathan Livingston Seagull	207
I'm sad	367
Iron -> Flesh	15
I Seldom Pray to Rabies	220
It is the Wine of Sin	358
It's Hard to be Happy as a Bohemian	186
I will not judge you when we sit across from each other in the silence	254

J

Jenő's Ghost, The Unfinished Sympathy	209
John Lamb	153
Johnny 5 Fingers	175

K

Kaiju Nightmare	179
Kontinentális Talapzat	25

L

Last Year is Swimming in a Cup of Blood	253

Last Year I Had an Opportunity	•
Like Red Screaming from Home	250
Lowballgeddon	152

M

Maybe not	365
Maybe They're a fan.	•
Mr. Kite's Worsted	202
Muffin McWorms	165
My Angry Days	251

N

Naval	222

O

O Galileo Where Art Thou Satellites	200
Oh God I've Peaked!!!	242
Old Row Redux	195
Out Back to Worth into the Mind	237

P

Posthumous Books	289
Praise for Világos	290
Probably not	366

R

release	368
Remember your experience	•

S

Scaramouch Kazoo	183
Secret texts of a Horror Story	232
Song of the Dawn	167
Song of the Morning	168
Sorozás	13
Strong and Tall and Missing	235
Sunny Domino	157
Superman's Blackout	177
Sweet Voiced Melodies	18

T

Take Out a Gun and Blow off your Foot	231
The Endless Exploding Lights	210
The Flesh Eating Bionic Squirrel	164
The Giant Mouth/The Typhoon	159
The Hypochondriac	161
The Last Night was the Last Night not the First	239
The Lightning Klaxon Riding Shotgun	194
The Magnetic Fields at Zero Gravity	178
The Millionaire Fire Fight	211
The New Gambit / The Koalabat	193
The Night Before	155
There All Right	234
The Red Child	150
The Road To Wrestlemania	215
The Rockons	188
The Side of the Pool	169

The Wine of Sin is Here	356
This One's Tiny Friend	241
those who got mummified to be left alone	248
Three Eight Songs	201
Three Starving	252
Tried to Remember the Party	245

V

Verisimilitude	24

W

Waiting for the Show to go on	219
Well-Fermented Crust	198
We're One Shot Waiting For the Light/Battle In The Skies	263
Why do men sleep?	
Wine and Plum Evil	359
Wolfpack Beats Per Minute	212
Work.	

Y

Year After Year Onwards	350
You Killed My Cousin in a Drive-by	214
Young Knuckle	156

LAY OUT YOUR PSEUDONYM

www.ingramcontent.com/pod-product-compliance
Lightning Source LLC
Chambersburg PA
CBHW020322170426
43200CB00006B/240